Ordinary Woman
Extraordinary Life

By Irma Pallas

Copyright© 2012 by Irma Pallas. All rights reserved.

No part of this book may be reproduced, stored in a retrieval system, or transmitted by any means, electronic, mechanical, photocopying, recording or otherwise, without written permission from the author.

ISBN: 978-0-9851813-2-1

LOGAN SQUARE PRESS
ALBUQUERQUE, NEW MEXICO
USA

Contents

Editor's Note   v
Introduction   viii
Word from the Author   x
Prefix: In Memory   xii

Part One Overcoming Hardship   1
1. War in the Eyes of a Child   3
2. Worclaw, Part One - Relocation   7
3. Wrocław, Part Two - In Memory of my Teacher Pani Janina   14
4. Search for a Better Life - The Wonderland Germany   20
5. The Dearest Person in My Life - Grandma   26
6. Love and Sorrow for a Mother   32
7. The Father I Never Knew   45
8. Relationship - Touching Moment   51

Part Two - The Rough Road Ahead   56
9. Hamburg - My Second Home   57
10. Search for a Father Replacement   63
11. Romance with a Show-off Person   69
12. Brazilian Connection   74
13. Return to the Roots in 1969   79
14. The Moscow Love Story   83
15. Two Months in Leningrad   89
16. Assignment in Poland Part One   93
17. Assignment in Poland Part Two - The Spy Affair   102
18. Assignment in Poland Part Three - My Friend Bozena   105

Part Three - Start of a Better and Happier Life   109
19. Chicago Part One - You must Love the City   110
20. Chicago Part Two - Stanley Pisz   120
21. People to be Remembered   128
22. Blind Date - Meet the Con man   133
23. Rudi - Successful Marriage   137
24. Coco - In Memory of a Companion   143
25. Family Unifications   148

26. Miracle - A New Family Found in 2004	152
27. First Anniversary with the Children in 2005	165
28. Europe Trip with the Children in 2006	169
29. The Wedding and First Grandchild	181
30. Friends for Life	188
Conclusion	197

Editor's Note

It seems insulting to call someone "ordinary."

After all, we are all different and unique and have had our own battles with life and fascinating stories to tell. All our lives are filled with everything from trauma, to joy, tragedy, boredom, failures, bad choices, lousy marriages, unfulfilled dreams, bad jobs, optimism, laughter, love and triumph.

Most of us don't get a chance to tell those stories because we're not part of this celebrity-obsessed culture in which we live. We have jobs to go to every day, bills to pay and families to raise, and camera crews never beat down our doors to sensationalize and breathlessly report on our addictions, divorces, failures and successes.

Movie stars, politicians and athletes get all the attention, and all we're left with is reading or watching about how another multimillionaire overcame yet another series of self-inflicted wounds.

It is in those "ordinary" lives, though, that life is waged every single day and where true inspiration comes from. Every day our fellow "ordinary" neighbors, co-workers and colleagues are battling life, overcoming adversity and succeeding. Their successes—finding a lost relative, reconnecting with a friend or having the courage to get out of a bad marriage—are small and insignificant to the celebrity-obsessed media. But to those "ordinary" people, those successes are monumental.

Irma Pallas isn't famous. She has worked as a tour guide in Europe and the old Soviet Union, as an employee for the West German Embassy in Warsaw, at the Consulate General in Chicago and for machine tool companies in the U.S. and Germany.

Her life, though, has been interesting. She was born in 1941 in a part of Poland that had been conquered by the Nazis. Her father, part of the German security forces, was killed on the Eastern Front.

She watched the Soviet Army roll over the Nazis and reconquer Poland. At the end of the war, her family was "stateless," neither Polish nor German. Her mother and grandparents struggled to reunite with family members in West Germany after the war, which they did in 1955.

From there, Irma's life became a wild rollercoaster ride with bad marriages and relationships, depression, joy, love, spies, an estrangement from her mother and much more. At one point, Irma, depressed, made the decision to end up in the street. She never did it, as life intervened and sent her on a different course. Her story is filled with those "ordinary" heartbreaks: guys who are jerks, lost dogs and a mother searching the bars of Hamburg for her drug-addict son while carrying a shopping bag with a pair of clean underwear for him.

There's intrigue. The Polish Secret Service followed Irma wherever she went in Warsaw, and assisted her when locals purposely caused car crashes in an attempt to get money from westerners.

There's humor, like the Brit she once dated who used Super Glue to keep his bad teeth attached to his gums.

And there's kindness—teachers who made sure the young girl completed her studies and found the strength to carry on in the face of adversity; friends who showed up at her apartment doors to lend their ears when she was depressed and take her to dinners and the opera when she was struggling financially; Polish security officers who, at the Height of the Cold War, walked an employee of the West German government to her apartment and surveyed the area for lurking intruders; and a Russian gentleman who, seeing a young woman walking alone in a Leningrad park at 2 a.m., escorted her safely to her hotel and kissed her hand in departure as a gentlemanly sign of respect.

In 1974 Irma came to the U.S. as an employee of the West German Consulate, and, for the most part, stayed. She has seen a good portion of the world in her travels and jobs.

Irma's story is like all of ours. She has had good and bad times, and at seventy-years-old, is still standing. Actually, she's doing more than that; she's celebrating and enjoying life. She has gotten through the tough times and has learned that real happiness comes from the "ordinary" things—taking a walk with her husband Rudi, picking up the phone and calling a friend, sending someone a card and taking vacations with Rudi's children and their spouses.

Irma knows that it's those ordinary pleasures that make for an extraordinary life.

Dennis Domrzalski
Logan Square Press

Introduction

Writing an autobiography has often meant writing down the facts of one's life without recording any feelings. When I started to write my story, I learned to understand how to portray people and events, as well as my thoughts and responses to all those people and events.

Quite often I heard the advice, "Write what you know. Actual events from your past can become the key to developing writing skills." It was easier said than done. I had to learn to be confident of my own identity and ability to explain where I had lived and what I had lived for.

Learning writing skills and techniques did not come easy. I was missing "helpers" who were willing to explain and develop my awareness about language structure instead of criticizing. I speak several languages, and English is not my first. I had several drafts started, and only in the last one did I realize how much attention must be paid to spelling, structure and punctuation.

I started the autobiography more than five years ago. Several times it ended up in my desk drawer due to a lack of time or the drive to continue. But when vivid memories came to me, I rushed to my desk and made notes so I would not miss or forget them. Suddenly, I discovered that my life was filled with joy, sadness, hardship, and the worst of all, loneliness. I realized that I missed my childhood which I spent in Salesia, Poland; my friends, my teacher, and even the very simple life after the World War II.

We lived behind the Iron Curtain, communicated only with relatives in the West, but had no idea what life would be in West Germany. My family and I had difficulties in adjusting to the lifestyle and different mentality. I also finally realized how I loved the country I came from and how I never forgot my heritage. I know now that I had friends for life who are still there and where I am welcome any time.

Through the process of writing my story I found dear friends and helpers who helped and encouraged me to continue with this autobiography, and to whom I address my gratitude.

Finally, I often thought, "Why would anyone want to read about me, Irma Pallas? I'm not famous and have never aspired to fame or celebrity. I'm just an ordinary human being."

Then I realized that most everybody on this planet is like me. Ninety-nine percent of us aren't famous. So many of us have had bad marriages, lousy role models, a lack of emotional support and bad times. We want to shed the depression and live with joy and happiness. I managed through my bad times and have found love, laughter and joy in life. I know now that I survived because, along the way, I found wonderful and "ordinary" people who cared enough to help another human being.

I hope that my story will inspire other "ordinary" people who have had bad times and who are looking for encouragement to master their lives in good and bad times.

With joy, hope, love and gratitude,

Irma Pallas

Word from the Author

I decided to become an American citizen, not because I needed the immigration papers, but because of the feeling that this country would be my second homeland. I had been here for ten years, met many people, made friends, and most of all, felt comfortable and secure. It was a great moment for me when I first recited the Pledge of Allegiance and later received the Certificate of Citizenship. That happened in October 1985. At that time, I knew for certain that I would not return to West Germany where my family lived and still lives.

The city of Chicago contributed a lot to my decision. I felt welcomed there. During the stage of settling down, I had contact with people from several ethnic groups, particularly with Polish people. I got acquainted with people who came to this country either after World War II, or later when the political and economic situation in the home country forced them to immigrate, legally or illegally, to find a job to support their families back home.

Polish workmanship was known as one of the best in America, as well as in Western Europe. Poles are skillful, have a positive attitude and are eager to succeed. Unfortunately, often they were misjudged and denigrated. They became the object of stupid jokes.

Since leaving Poland in 1955, I have visited the country on several occasions. On each visit, I saw improvements, especially in big cities, but also in the outskirts as well as in smaller towns.

With the political changes in Poland, people's ambitions rose and they were willing to work on rebuilding historical sites and cleaning up old, dirty and crumbling facades. It was an eye opener when I visited Poland in May 2011. I was stunned at how much everything had changed. It was exciting to be there, and it felt good. I was home, a better one than so many years before. The improvements have opened the door to the business world and visitors from all over the world.

I took the chance to visit friends I had not seen for many years. While they used to struggle in the older times, I was happy to see them doing well. They had bought condominiums or houses, and had secured a comfortable life. But nothing came to them easily. They worked hard, and now that they are partially retired, they have the benefits of enjoying themselves and travelling without the restrictions that were imposed by the Communists.

We all aged with the years, but got wiser in many things. We did not forget each other over the years, and are determined to cherish our friendship no matter how far away we are from each other.

In Memory and Dedication

This biography is dedicated to several people some of whom are not with us today but who helped me overcome obstacles: Robert Beck, Josef Strasberger, Horst Cohn, and to my dear friends with whom I cherish a deep and wonderful friendship: Beatrice Stillman, Bozena Paprocka, Teresa Staron-Lamowska and Marilyn Leben

Last but not least, I would like to thank my aunt, Hanna Preissner, in Kiel, Germany, who welcomed me into her house when I was fifteen. She treated me as if I was her own daughter. There I found warmth, love and sincerity.

Thank you to all.

Part One
Overcoming Hardship

Chapter 1
War in the Eyes of a Child

I was not quite four years old when World War II began to reach its end phase with the worst and most horrible effects. The following is what I learned as the war came to an end.

The Russian Army, together with Polish troops, forced the German occupiers back toward the west, while rolling though the occupied territories along the way. One of those territories was Salesia, the eastern part of the Third Reich. Today it is the western part of Poland.

Most of the Russian soldiers were very young and inexperienced. They originated from the poorest families and had little education. For the first time in their lives, they came in contact with a more cultured world, and it was very overwhelming to them. They invaded homes and robbed and mistreated families. The first things that caught their eyes were watches. Their arms were covered with ladies' and men's watches. My mother gave them an alarm clock in exchange for a can of sausages. Where they got the sausages from we did not know. Alcohol was the next item they looked for. They got drunk, danced on tables, and other costly furniture. They even dressed in women's nightgowns and marched through the streets and sang loud Russian songs.

Polish soldiers also invaded homes and behaved very brutally. For example, while mother was feeding us one day, one of the soldiers lifted his rifle with the intention of smashing her head. My sister and I screamed so loud that it brought him to his senses.

Meanwhile, other Polish soldiers robbed our grandparents' apartment. They stole all their silver and other valuable items, and smashed their piano and other furniture. They were in a terrible rage.

During the days and at nights, allied bombers circled the city, Hindenburg, (today Zabrze). The noise told us that the alarm sirens would soon be heard. Everybody looked for shelter, and we did it as well. Our cellar was very stable and served as a shelter. Mother rolled us up in a featherbed and pushed it down the stairs because we were not able to run. Grandmother brought us to safety just as a bomb hit our house. It landed in the bathtub of the upper apartment where mother had just soaked laundry, thus avoiding an explosion. The impact ripped a big hole into the outside wall, sending debris down to the lower floors.

My grandparents' apartment, which was one story below, was covered with dust and dirt. Grandpa, who was eating his breakfast, jumped away at the last moment when he heard the dull noise and escaped serious injury.

The misery started from that moment. Germans were not allowed to speak their native language. Following Germany's capitulation on May 8, 1945, food, and daily necessities were obtainable only with food stamps.

Our good fortune was the vegetable garden which my grandparents still maintained. Carrots and potatoes were covered with sand in the sandbox to protect them from cold temperatures during the winter. In the backyard, Grandpa kept several rabbits. As long as they were small, we kids could play with them. Later on, they served as our meals, since no meat was available.

We were not able to leave our homeland, which now belonged to Poland. Most of our relatives were in West Germany. The borders were closed, and we needed to adjust to the new situation. Suddenly, we realized what the "Iron Curtain" meant. All remaining Germans were forced to accept Polish citizenship. However, our family refused it. From that moment on our status was "stateless," which meant that we came from nowhere, and did not belong to anyone. We didn't belong to Germany or to Poland. History had repeated itself again. In previous centuries, Poland had often been occupied and divided, which made people insecure and ask, "Who am I?" and "Where do I belong?"

My mother and grandparents purposely refused the Polish citizenship, hoping that a family reunion would happen with the family in West Germany. The next ten years were very difficult. Grandfather had been imprisoned for several months because Polish authorities suspected that he had been a member of the Nazi Party. Fortunately, witnesses who had known him for years were able to prove the contrary.

Since my father was killed on the Eastern Front in 1942, mother was forced to find a job to keep us going. Father was captain of the German Police Boarder Enforcement, and due to an administrative mistake, his battalion was deployed to the Russian Front. He visited my godmother, Nurse Gertrud, in Riga before joining his fellow soldiers. He was killed by a shellfire on June 5, 1942, near Rogawka, Russia.

My grandfather, whose occupation was chimney sweeper, continued his work in the industrial area and contributed financially to our household. Grandmother took charge of the household and also cared for us children in the best way she could.

Because the use of the German language was forbidden, our friends and neighbors met in neutral places, such as in our garden or in parks where nobody could listen to the German language the adults were speaking.

As children, we picked up the Polish language quickly, which also helped mother to enroll us in the kindergarten, and later into grammar school. But in 1946, the situation worsened, and my grandfather decided that we should leave Zabrze immediately. Through friends a truck was hired, and during the night, one bed frame, pillows, blankets and personal items were quickly loaded. In no time we were on the way towards a small village, Grabin, where my grandfather's sister had a small farm house.

As we arrived there, we realized that we were not welcome. Aunt Anna did not keep close contact with her brother—my grandfather—and made our stay miserable. She was a mean woman, a widow who lived with her daughter of the same name. I remember that both were always dressed in dark or black dresses. Their home was dirty, bugs were all over, and no bathroom or proper sanitary equipment was available, causing me to get very sick. My legs were sore from insect bites and boils which resulted in open and bleeding wounds. Mother washed them with chamomile tea to keep dirt and further infection away. Mother contacted the Catholic priest, who was able to assist us during this time of transition. In the meantime, grandfather had moved to another city, Wrocław. There he found a job and we were supposed to follow him, but this took more than several months. Meanwhile, my sister, who was eighteen months older than me, enrolled in the grammar school which was located next to the church. There was only one classroom and one teacher. The teacher divided the students up according to their ages, and had to teach in shifts.

Finally, in late spring of 1947, we moved. Again a truck was organized and we were on our way towards the city of Breslau—today Wroclaw. We did not know what to expect. Also, we could not understand why it took so long for our grandfather to get us there. He, in the meantime, had a liaison with a woman, and therefore was preoccupied.

Chapter 2
Wrocław Part One – Relocation

As mentioned in the previous chapter, pursuit and harassment as well as imprisonment of my grandfather forced us to leave our birth city Hindenburg (today Zabrze) very discreetly one night in 1947. A loaded truck brought us to a village where we stayed with relatives for several months until Grandfather found work and a place to live in Wrocław. This city used to be German prior to WW II and, therefore, it was a target to be destroyed.

Wrocław is the capital of Lower Salesia, one of Poland's most populous regions, and it is located at the intersection of transcontinental routes linking Scandinavia with Southern Europe, and Western Europe with Ukraine. Situated on the Odra River, Wroclaw is known as the city of a hundred bridges. Its remarkable history is reflected in its architectural and artistic heritage. Its rapid development over the last decade has made Wroclaw one of Central Europe's most exciting cities. Visitors were moved by the church monuments located on an island surrounded by the river Odra.

In 1947, when entering the city, there were burned houses, ruins and damaged street. It was a sad welcome. The house facades, generally gray and full of gun holes, made a very depressing and devastating impression on us. And we thought that this city was supposed to give us shelter!

We stopped in front of a six-story apartment house. Next to it was a burned out house and we were afraid it would collapse at any time. It did indeed, and soon it was brought down. Because a high rate of unemployment existed, people were called for work, but this work meant to clean the bricks by hand and sort them out for reuse. Then those bricks were transported to the capital, Warsaw. It was priority for the Polish government to rebuild its capital.

Life went on in Wrocław. Only some streets were cleaned up and patched. We move and settled in on the sixth floor. There was no elevator, and no staircase light. Each floor accommodated four apartments. On the sixth floor there were two apartments, with two families sharing the bathroom. There was also an attic with access to the roof and a laundry drying loft. Between the ceiling and roof there was no insulation. Rats were racing at night.

The apartment itself consisted of two simple rooms, a little kitchen and a storage room. We were five people living in this small apartment. The arrangement was that one room served as a bedroom and the other as a living, dining and family room combined. Since we had only one bed (Grandfather's), it was necessary to organize bed frames with straw bags replacing the missing mattresses. We pulled the bed frames out of the surrounding ruins. We added two bed frames, and by that time we had three beds which had to be shared among five people. Each day we were looking for some "goodies" and necessities.

My sister and I were enrolled in the grammar school. Mother started to work at the hospital as a nurse assistant, and Grandpa continued his profession as a chimney sweeper. People liked him very much, therefore, companies supplied him with meat, sausages and other helpful items for us.

At school we made friends, and I was very lucky to be awarded each year for being one of the best students. In the afternoon, I was usually involved in soccer and handball games with classmates. During the summers we went swimming or did other sporting activities. But we also spent four weeks each year on our uncle's farm. Uncle Theofil was Mother's cousin.

The trip from Wrocław via Brzeg to Skoroszyce took us approximately four to five hours. From there our uncle picked us up with a horse-drawn vehicle and we continued about seven kilometers bumping around the pot holes. The trains at that time were not comfortable at all. Passenger trains were commuting only from big city to big city, therefore, often we had to take the cattle wagons. The reason to go to the farm, besides the fun we experienced, was to get more nutritional meals.

The farm consisted of a farmhouse with one room on the main floor where we all slept, and a kitchen with a manual water pump. The water came out of the well located in the hallway. The second floor had two small rooms, but nobody was sleeping there because the wooden floor was rotten and nobody could step on it. Immediately next to the farmhouse was the pig sty and cow shed connected, and above that the hayloft. There was also a corner which housed a chicken coop.

Two barns served for the harvested grain and for tooling, such as a plow and threshing machine. Everything was simple and primitive compared to present day equipment. Uncle Theofil had two horses, three cows and two pigs.

We had fun with the outhouse next to the dunghill. When using it we counted and observed spiders around us, not to mention the flies. We still laugh about it today.

During the days Uncle Theofil assigned chores to us. First we helped harvest hay, load it on the hay wagon, climbed on top of it, drove home and unloaded it to the hay loft. Another task was to tender the cows. We had to lead them to the pasture ground. Out of boredom we baked potatoes sticks over campfires. On rainy days we helped Aunt Otilie in the house. We learned how to churn butter and make farmers cheese.

The best was the bread and cake she baked. We had to bring the prepared bread dough and baking tins to the local bakery. There they had a huge oven. The use of the oven was assigned by the baker. Our aunt baked every week. My sister and I could hardly wait to pick up the fresh baked bread and cake. We started nibbling on the way home. It was just too tempting. Later we ate the bread with mustard spread, since cold cuts were not always available. The fresh baked bread we ate with butter and mustard. For us it was heavenly. Butchering was done only in winter. The meat was mostly made into sausages, ham and bacon, which were later smoked.

During the last two weeks of our stay we helped to harvest grain and bring it into the barns. The bundling was done by hand. The ties were made from straw prior to the harvest. Then the dried out bundles were loaded and brought in and unloaded into the barns. Later the grain was threshed, separated from the straw and the grain was brought to the mill. The straw, however, was stored and used in the cow and horse sheds.

Unfortunately, we learned later that our Uncle Theofil had a fatal accident. We were told that while he was repairing the threshing machine, his niece turned on by mistake the high-voltage power which killed him.

In 2002, my sister, mother and husband Rudi visited this farm. My aunt Otilie passed away some time ago. There was only the niece Hilde with her children living. In the meantime, both barns burned down.

It was heartbreaking to see how this little farm was run-down. Hilde had four children, three boys and one girl. One of the boys committed suicide; the other two have a mental illness which is controlled by medication. The daughter, Barbara, was the only healthy and hardworking person in the family. She carried on the responsibility for the household and her siblings. She married and divorced, but raised her two children in the best way she could and who are today are doing very well at school. After her mother passed away, she managed to get the farmhouse remodeled, and she proudly told me on the phone that they have now a nice and clean bathroom. Everything seemed to fall in place for her.

At that time the area was influenced by the Communist regime. Schools forced everyone to be a member of a youth group (similar to Boy/Girl scouts) with propaganda activities. On days such as May first (Labor Day in Europe) or May ninth (Capitulation/War end celebration), we had to participate in parades carrying signs and photos of Communist Party members. In schools, religion or prayers were not allowed. However, because Poland was a Catholic country, and bishops and cardinals were fighting for religious freedom, there was some improvement. Churches were crowded on Sundays and holidays.

Following seven years of grammar school, students continued for four years at a high school before enrolling in a university or technical college. The education standard was at a very high level. School hours were usually from 8.00 a.m. till 2.00 p.m., Monday through Saturday. Homework was given every day.

The public high schools were for Polish citizens only. Since we were marked "stateless," there was no chance for us to enroll.

Mother contacted a private school conducted by Catholic nuns, and my older sister Karin was accepted first, while I followed a year later.

The school rules were very strict. A uniform code had to be observed. Unfortunately, the tuition at this private school was very high and many parents were not able to afford it. Learning foreign languages was a must, and the Russian language was number one in the public schools, as well as in private schools. Additional languages were German or French in the public school, and French or Latin in private high schools.

Some of our grammar school friends who were Jewish had to struggle with the Communist system. Jewish people were not loved by their Polish neighbors. Some of the reasons were the intelligence and talents they were blessed with. Their ability to be in managing positions, such as bank and financial areas, was hated.

Their involvement in jewelry businesses and their trade skills with gold and diamonds were called "dirty business." The worst of all was their faith and temple activities. The Jewish people were harassed, and quite often imprisoned.

That happened to the Jewish mother of my girlfriend Marilyn. For several months her mother was in prison. One time I accompanied Marilyn to the courthouse. One room faced the prison side. Through the court window we communicated in sign language with Marilyn's mother. Marilyn had to drop out of school and take over the household. She cared for her small sister Sarah. Marilyn missed the last graduation year of the grammar school, and therefore, she could not enroll in a high school.

The year 1955 was an important year for me and my family. I enrolled in the private high school in September, and a few weeks later we celebrated the golden anniversary of our grandparents. Friends and family members joined the festivity in our small apartment. At that time we did not know that this would be the last family festivity in Wrocław. My grandmother was very fragile; she lost a lot of weight and suffered from Parkinson's disease, while my grandfather was in great shape. The marriage had not a happy one. He was a grumpy and angry man and he made the celebration very tense.

At first my grandfather did not want to participate in this family event, but finally my mother pressured him and everybody met in church for the blessing. My sister and I got for the first time new hairdos, and Mother furnished us with long taffeta dresses. Dinner was later served in the small apartment.

The political situation was very tense, and changes in the government were disputed. The German chancellor, Konrad Adenauer, visited Moscow, and the president of the German Red Cross, Professor Peter Weiss, went to Warsaw. The agenda for both gentlemen was to enforce family unification for German citizens. By accident our mother met Professor Weiss, who visited Wroclaw. He assured her that our family would be one of the first families to leave the country on the Red Cross train. We had to keep it as secret as possible. We were afraid that jealous neighbors or acquaintances would jeopardize it. Too many people of German descent tried same way as we did to be relocated to West Germany. They would not have understood why it was us and not them. We were afraid that badmouthing our family to officials, would lead to a failure in getting out of Poland.

At the end of 1955 we received the paperwork and started to pack. It was a stressful time. Many things were left behind, such as furniture and kitchen supplies. Mother distributed money and gifts to people who helped us to leave the town. The trip took us by special truck to Szczecin, a port on the Baltic Sea. There was a camp, where the chosen families gathered in order to embark the Red Cross train which brought us to the West. Exactly one year later we learned that the new Polish government had forced all Jewish people out of the country. My friends Marilyn and Rita and their families, were among the Jewish people who left, either to Israel or Austria. Many years later we found each other in Vienna and the United States.

Chapter 3
Wrocław Part Two - In Memory of my Teacher Pani Janina

In April 2011 a phone call from Poland informed us that my former elementary school teacher, Pani Janina Lupaczyk, had passed away after a ten years of illness. Her daughter Marta gave us this sad news, which also came as a relief. We knew how difficult those years had been. During the last years a nurse had to be with Pani Janina around-the-clock. Pani Janina had injured her head when she fell down some stairs. From then on she slowly lost functions. She did not recover from her injuries and declined more and more. I remember her as a very lively, bright and articulate lady who was born on November 7, 1913 in Grodno, a town located today in Belarus, part of the former Soviet Union, which once belonged to the eastern part of Poland. She married her husband Alexander on August 1, 1939. He passed away on February 28, 1982. He had suffered a stroke and medical assistance had come too late. The couple had one daughter, Marta, who was born on January 12, 1953, and who married her husband Jurek on November 23, 1974. Two granddaughters extended their small family. Ula was born on April 4, 1975, and Dorka was born on February 12, 1980.

 The last time I saw Pani Janina was when my mother and my sister accompanied my husband Rudi and me to Wroclaw. We fulfilled my mother's wish to once more to see the place that she called her home. Unfortunately, we did not realize at the time that her dementia had already kicked in, as she did not recognize places where she used to work and live.

I remember Pani Janina from the time I was enrolled to the first grade class in 1947. The war experience and relocations made me shy and anxious to deal with new environments and people. We settled down in Wroclaw, and the elementary school happened to be across the street. My grandmother was able to see me in the classroom when she looked out the window of our sixth floor apartment.

My school enrollment papers were checked and approved. I knew that my life would change drastically. We had already experienced difficulties with our documents, which indicated that we were Staatenlos, which meant to be without citizenship. Polish authorities had tried to force my family to acknowledge Polish citizenship, however, we declined, hoping that one day we would be reunited with our family in West Germany. After the war the borders had been moved and the area we used to live in, and which once had belonged to Germany, was now declared Polish. The area where Pani Janina originated from used to be Polish and is now Russian. She, as well as many others, was forced to relocate and move to the western part of present-day Poland.

At home we spoke German. The Polish language was difficult for me. Children, as we know, can be very rude and did not understand the circumstances of my troubles. They made fun of me and called me "Szwabka," which was a slander directed at Germans.

Here Pani Janina stepped in as a guardian. She tried to explain to the children what it felt like to be relocated, losing your home and having to learn a new language. She helped me to ignore such behavior or fight it. Several times she came to my rescue when she caught me crying and offered me advice on how to overcome nastiness and to concentrate on my learning. I never forgot her saying, "with friendliness you will win over your enemies."

Those basic steps helped me to concentrate on my studies, and soon I was one of the advanced students, not only in the first, or second grades, but also in the higher grade classes. I also received book awards at each of the end-of-the-school-year ceremonies. Also I proved how tough I could be. If necessary, I was not shy to fight with boys, but also showed them my ability in playing either soccer or handball. Most of the time I played in goal.

I remember when Pani Janina got very sick and had to stay home. I organized with some school friends a home visit and we brought her flowers and a fruit basket which was difficult to come by. She never forgot it and mentioned it often to my mother or grandfather when they attended teacher-parent meetings. My grandfather always came home beaming because he was very proud to hear good news. Since I loved geography and math, Pani Janina assigned me to help fellow students to brush up on their learning so they could pass the final tests.

To have to say goodbye to her when the time came to leave the country was heartbreaking and very emotional for us. I was losing a guardian and a friend who always found a moment to lend an ear or a shoulder to cry on, but we promised to each other to stay in touch.

The first three years in Germany were very tough. During the years in Poland I had lost the ability to communicate in German. Therefore, I had a hard time socializing with other students and adjusting to a different lifestyle. At the time we left Poland, the country's economy and lifestyle was very poor with a lot of limitations in regard to food and other necessities. In Germany, on the other hand, stores were flooded with merchandise and supermarkets had fruits I had never seen. Often I had the feeling of not being welcomed. Due to a different mentality, people were not eager to offer a helping hand. We were still known as refugees with no place in that society. In my letters to Pani Janina I complained many times to her about it. In her in response she asked me to be patient and give it some time. I had to admit that our correspondence kept the Polish language alive in me, at least in reading and writing. There was no one I could converse with, and I was afraid that over time the language would fade. My two girlfriends, Maryla and Rita, had left the country as well, one to Israel, the other to the Czech Republic, and later to Austria. Only after ten years did I find them and we started communicating with each other.

In 1969 I was able to book a holiday return trip to Poland. The program covered only Warsaw and surroundings including sightseeing, theater events and New Year's Eve celebrations. Prior to booking the trip I made sure I could spare one day and visit Pani Janina in Wroclaw. I informed her over the phone of the details of my arrival by train. It was supposed to be a secret trip because foreigners were being watched by the authorities. Yes, I was very nervous. The husband of Pani Janina met me at the station and we took a taxi to go to her home. I was exhausted and they insisted that I take a two-hour nap. Afterwards, we had a few hours to catch up with each other before I had to return.

I met Marta, the daughter of my teacher who had just turned sixteen. Marta was a very bright and pleasant young lady who later became a very close friend. They all accompanied me the next day to the train station and I promised to visit them again, not knowing when that might be.

I never imagined that my professional career would ever bring me back to Poland. However, fate would have it that in 1972 I did return to Poland as an employee for the German Trade Mission, which later became the Embassy of the West German Republic. And yes, I had to pass a test as the translator for the German/Polish and Polish/German language.

During my two-year term in Warsaw I visited Wroclaw often and was able to supply the family with non-perishable food items and clothing for their daughter.

My term in Warsaw ended after two years when I received a transfer notice to Chicago. There were quick goodbyes again. While being in Chicago our communication continued for seventeen years. During this time I learned that Marta had married in 1974, the granddaughters were born, and that the husband of Pani Janina had died in 1983. I was very sad at not being able to participate in those happy, but also sad, events. That family was always close to my heart.

In 1991 my husband and I were transferred to Germany on business. Since I told Rudi so much about Wroclaw and the family of my previous teacher, he was eager to visit this city as well as to meet the family. We drove there by car and stayed for a few days of sightseeing, visiting my old school and talking about old times. We happened to meet the school principal, who welcomed us and was exited to show us the handwritten school records. Surprise, surprise, there was my class, our teacher and my name mentioned. I was very touched. We talked about that with my teacher over a nice dinner. Even though she was already retired, she was still very alert and remembered many of the funny stories.

During this visit we invited her granddaughters to come to Germany and spend their summer vacation with us. They came each of the following three years.

We played school teaching them German and English, and they earned money by helping in the household and caring for our dog. We had the best time, and even today we talk about that and laugh about some mishaps.

As mentioned above, Pani Janina injured herself in 2001 and needed constant care. During one of our last visits she did not recognize me and faded into her own world. We all kept her in our prayers and hoped for a quick end, which finally came in April 2011. Our recent visit to Poland, and a memorial service for her, was the last way to honor her goodness and sincerity. May she rest in peace.

Chapter 4
Search for a Better Life
The Wonderland Germany

Shortly before Christmas in 1955, our family and many others arrived with the Red Cross train in Friedland, West Germany. It was the very first attempt to bring families together that had been torn apart by the war. Friedland had established the very first refugee camp, which served to welcome people from the Eastern European countries.

We all had to pass health exams, register as refugees and receive the necessary instructions. We stayed in this temporary camp for only few days. We children found the offered food different compared to what we were used to. We got fruits which we had never seen, such as bananas, and a lot of sweets. It was the Christmas season. I remember getting sick from this food as my stomach could not handle it.

Our uncle George and his wife Ingeborg from Frankfurt came to greet us. They, of course, did not realize how poorly we looked and how we were dressed. They seemed to be ashamed to identify themselves as being related to us.

Suddenly, there was the rude awakening. My grandmother, who used to tell us the most wonderful stories about this country, experienced her first disappointment. She was very fragile and exhausted; she could not even keep a conversation going. Everything was overwhelming, looked different, and all the actions and commotions were too much to absorb. My uncle and aunt were under tremendous pressure since their only child—son Mathias—was dying of Leukemia, and they left him temporarily with a nurse at home.

After all formalities were concluded, our trip continued towards the Baltic Sea, at the northern part of West Germany. We took the train at the central station in Goettingen and got off in Luebeck, where our uncle Theo, my mother's older brother, was supposed to expect us. Uncle Theo was a surgeon who was residing with his family in the town of Neustadt. We were told that he would pick us up at the train station. When we arrived and waited for him, we did not know where to look for him. So many years had passed, people had aged and appearances had changed. He did not recognize our little group. He passed us several times until Mother called his name. It must have been the greatest shock in his life.

Uncle Theo was accompanied by an older gentleman, Mr. Reese, who used to go hunting with him. Both came with uncle's car, a Mercedes. We were too many people to fit in this car. Therefore, my sister and Mr. Reese had to take the train. On the way home I got sick again in my stomach, but my uncle was prepared, he had enough paper towels in his car.

Finally we arrived at home. My uncle had a big apartment within the clinic area and additional rooms had been made available to accommodate us. In the meantime, a three-story, one-family house was in the process of being built, which was ready by the end of 1956.

My aunt Hanna assumed that we would have difficulties in adjusting to different food, so she prepared a rice dish, which we did not like very much. She tried very hard to make us feel welcome. Aunt Hanna and Uncle Theo had three children from the age range of one year, two-and-a-half, and the oldest, five. It was not always easy for her to be the wife of a famous surgeon with added responsibilities. Today I am proud to say that nobody was as dedicated to the family as my aunt, even now in the age of ninety-two!

Our very first Christmas in Germany was special and different. My aunt made sure that we got new clothes and had all the other necessary daily items. Suddenly we became such a big family! The most difficult and frustrating experience was communicating in the German language. We used to speak Polish and understood some German, but to speak in German was very different. I was very shy and hesitant in regard to the German language. Our little cousins, whom I had to baby sit, forced us to speak in German.

My aunt arranged for us to be enrolled in the middle school for a few months until a private school had been found. In April 1956, the Secretary of Culture in Bonn realized that refugees with different native languages were a big problem. There were no teachers available with the knowledge of a different language. The schools had to be prepared, and the teachers trained in how to handle students like us. Finally, we were accepted into a private Catholic high school.

This private school was in Vechta, a town famous for various schools and prisons, and was a Catholic influenced area. This high school was a boarding school conducted by nuns. My sister and I were separated due to different class levels. We did not see each other often; it was not allowed, and I felt very lonely. There was a communication problem between the teacher and myself. I was very good in math, biology, physics, geography and chemistry, however, German, English and French were out of my range. I felt left out and was bored.

I played "mailman" between girl students and the boys, whose boarding school was not too far away. Before long I was caught. My mother was informed that I should be discharged immediately. I thought, "Thank God!" It was time for me to go. I just couldn't stand to be there, and couldn't make any friends.

My sister was lucky since she could finish the school with a knowledge of the Russian language. There was an older teacher who originated from the same area in Poland as we did. He knew Russian perfectly and received permission to give my sister the final exam in Russian instead of English.

There was no other solution than to return to the town where my uncle Theo was residing. I was glad to be back with my grandmother, whom I loved and adored. She, in the meantime, was very frail and sick and lost her will to live.

My mother in the meantime had to find a job, which was not easy. She began to attend seminars and enrolled in training sessions for the Red Cross in Bonn. At the beginning, money was a big issue, therefore, traveling to see us was out of question. For a long time Mother had to rent a room in Bonn with families who advertised availability. I hardly saw her, lost almost all contact and started to be estranged.

In Neustadt I enrolled back to the middle school and was lucky to have wonderful and understanding teachers. They helped me each step of the way. Not only did they help me with my school work, but they supported me emotionally as well. In addition to my school work, which included learning German, I helped my aunt Hanna to care for my grandmother until she died. I also helped with the household and cared for my cousins, who were by then nine, seven and five.

A retired teacher was a tutor who helped me to catch up with the German language and history as it was taught at school. When the final exams approached, we needed to submit an assignment with a voluntarily chosen subject. The teacher suggested that I turn in an assignment on "Salesia my Homeland." The request was to be handwritten, nineteen letter-size pages. I turned in fifty handwritten pages!

My uncle Theo had a good reputation as a surgeon. He worked long hours but hardly got involved in family matters. He was particularly rude towards me, and I had the feeling of being an intruder in his household. Whenever he knew that our school class had a test he would greet me with the negative remark: "You did not pass it, isn't it?" It didn't matter whether I passed or not, he always said the same thing. It was discouraging for me.

My aunt Hanna tried to support me, but often we had to lie in order to avoid unpleasant discussions with my uncle. He either ignored or badmouthed me, often in front of other people. During his home parties I felt like a servant. I had to offer champagne, wine or snacks to guests. My uncle made fun of me and forced me to make a curtsey. Those were his stupid jokes.

As time went by, he abused me emotionally and sexually. I found support in my teachers. My mother was far away, and when I mentioned the abuse to her, she did not believe me. I was not able to talk to my aunt about it either. She was a wonderful and warm person, and I couldn't find the courage to tell her what was happening. She later found out that her so famous surgeon husband had an affair with a prostitute. How long it was going on, we do not know. His changed behavior and his leaving the house in the evening made my aunt suspicions. She followed him once, was hiding behind the bushes in front of the house in which he entered and made only a noise which scared him off. Later, the closest friends confirmed to my aunt that they already knew about this liaison.

A strange lady intruded during a dinner party at a friend's house and directed a question to my aunt, "Do you know whom your husband is visiting in the evening hours?"

From that moment, Uncle Theo stood up and tried to force my aunt to leave the house and to go home. My Aunt Hanna, however, bless her heart, remained sitting and continued to enjoy the evening. She did not pay any attention to my uncle who then left. All his doing almost destroyed his carrier as well as the marriage.

After graduating high school, I decided to participate in training as a nurse assistant. I needed this training prior to enrollment into the medical school in Hamburg. This training took place in a hospital located in the town Papenburg. I stayed there for six months and I loved caring for sick people. I worked long hours, and several times also did night shifts. To this day I am still sometimes sorry for not becoming a nurse.

From there on, I got wiser, got adjusted to the western world and had a more positive outlook for the future.

In 1959, I had to choose the next educational step and decided to go to medical school. First I wanted to be a chemical lab technician, but then I decided for the profession of medical-technical assistant. That covered the area of clinical laboratories, pathology, bacteriology, chemistry, photography and radiotherapy.

The medical school in Hamburg was affiliated with one of the biggest hospitals in the city, and was a very well-known institution with strong demands. My sister, in the meantime, was involved in chemistry and finished her education in Kassel.

Because my mother could not afford very much pocket money to support us, I worked as an hourly helper in the shipping/receiving department on weekends at the publishing house of Der Spiegel and earned some money. I donated blood for a wonderful breakfast consisting of a boiled egg, cold cut, orange juice and milk, and also received thirty Deutschmarks pocket money. I donated blood six times, but had to stop because I got anemic. Quite often there were ups and downs; but many times I experienced having a guardian angel helping me out of distress. I learned to cherish friendship and be thankful for every new day.

Chapter 5
The Dearest Person in my Life

February 28, 1958, is a day I will never forget. That was the day I said goodbye to my grandmother Maria, whom I mourned for ten years after her death. I've visited her grave on a regular basis since then. If I needed help or was sad, I would talk to her as if she was my guardian angel. Therefore, I decided to dedicate this chapter to her.

Grandmother was born in 1882 in Wesel, a town located in the Rhine River area in the western part of Germany. As I understood, she had a very happy childhood and loving parents, but I don't remember them since I was too small when my mother, my sister and I visited them.

My grandmother fell in love with grandfather Emanuel. His occupation at that time was a chimney-sweeper—a very important job, especially in the industrial areas. He came from Salesia, the most eastern part of Germany which now is part of Poland. The lovebirds married and moved to Hindenburg (today Zabrze), a city with heavy industry such as coal mines and metallurgical plants. They had six children; three boys and three girls. One of the boys died when he was just one year old. The older of the remaining two boys, Theo, became a surgeon, and his brother George went into business. One of the girls, Maria, who was born illegitimate, specialized in health care apparels and later health food distribution. As my grandfather requested, the other girls, my aunt Hedwig, and my mother Lucia, had to stay home and be "kitchen oriented." My aunt did not agree with this and left her parents' home to search for a life of her own. My mother—the most spoiled child—remained with her parents even after she married my father in 1937.

My grandparents owned a four-story, red brick apartment building on a corner lot in Zabrze. My parents occupied an apartment on the third floor, while my grandparents' apartment was on the second floor. In 1940, my sister was born and I showed up in 1941. These were already the second and third years of World War II. My father belonged to a law enforcement unit connected to the military, and therefore, he hardly was home. Unfortunately, in June 1942, he was killed in the line of duty in Russia, and my mother's world fell apart. She took work in a hospital where she worked day and/or night shifts.

Grandmother became our guardian and babysitter, a job she did with unbelievable dedication and patience. She took us to the playgrounds and watched us as we worked in our vegetable garden which supplied us with food and fruits.

While we were growing up, each of us developed a different temperament and personality, which was not always easy on Grandma. My sister, who was spoiled by our mother, was fresh, stubborn, but also funny, while I enjoyed playing with danger. One day my little velvet dress caught fire, and at the last moment Grandmother rescued me by putting the flames out with her naked hand. Another time, I fell into a well in our garden. My sister came to the rescue. She was next to me when it happened, and held my legs and screamed for help. Again, my grandparents came to rescue me. There were many more incidents like that, but thankfully, I survived them without any harm.

The war's final years, 1944 and 1945, were terrible for us. Polish and Russian soldiers chased the German Army back to Berlin. On the way, they robbed and mistreated families, and we were victimized as well. The Polish gendarmerie imprisoned my grandfather under the suspicion that he might have been a member of the Nazi Party. They never did a background search on him. If they would have investigated, they would have learned that part of Grandfather's family was of Polish descent. We were not allowed to speak German. My grandmother managed to keep our small family intact, and she also helped a Jewish family to escape from the worst situations.

Grandpa was released in 1946, and there was no reason for us to remain in Zabrze. We had to move very quickly. A neighbor's daughter, who was dating a very nice Russian officer, helped us with a truck and driver, and we left at night. We had few stops on the way before we came to our final destination in Wroclaw several weeks later. During a temporary stay with relatives in the village of Grabin, I got sick from the dirt and bugs we encountered. Mother and Grandmother took turns washing me with chamomile tea until my bites and boils healed.

Finally, in 1947, my grandfather found a job and an apartment in Wroclaw, located in the northern part of Salesia. This was supposed to be our permanent home. The apartment was on the sixth floor and consisted of two rooms, a small kitchen with an old fashioned stove, no bathroom, and a common toilet we shared with our neighbors.

To keep our apartment warm, we had to carry coal from the cellar up to the sixth floor. Sometimes we stole wood from the backyard where a carpentry company stored its material. Grandmother took care of the household. She made sure that we had clean clothes, proper meals and did our homework. The school was across the street from our home, and during breaks, the students waved to Grandma when she looked out her window. She was loved by everyone and never complained about her hardships. We tried to ease her daily tasks and did the shopping, which meant standing in long lines hoping for a pound of butter, sugar or other necessities. Often we came home crying and empty-handed because the stores didn't have enough merchandise..

Grandma's strength was based on her hope that one day our situation would change. She told us about a better world and things she remembered from her past. Everything was good and cheap at that time. Her only wish was to be reunited with our family in West Germany. We also knew that the family in West Germany tried very hard to obtain visas for us. The Iron Curtain had been imposed on us after the war, and made those efforts very difficult.

In the meantime, Grandma had to overcome the hardship with my grandfather, Opa, who was not always easy to deal with. His temper and moods changed from day to day. He worked hard, but he kept us, including our grandmother, under a strict regimen. It was difficult enough because the five of us shared the small apartment. Not having the space to get away from Opa's screaming, cursing and violent acts towards Grandmother was the hardest thing. Opa did not give Grandmother a household allowance, but she found out where he hid his money. Then she took some from it and hid it herself. It was a constant struggle. It got worse when Grandmother learned about his affair with a lady in her fifties and confronted him. Opa often hit Grandmother in the face. Once, when he farted without excusing himself, I called him a pig. He almost killed me for that. My little grandmother got angry and said, "If you touch this child I will throw the chair at your head." She had finally stood up to him. I loved her for that and tried to always be around in order to protect and help her. I did not feel like a child anymore, on the contrary, I felt like a protector.

Finally, in December 1955, we were able to leave the country via a Red Cross train. Again, we could take only our personal items, so we distributed furniture and other things among our neighbors. From the remaining money, Mother and Grandmother bought jewelry, which we hid in our shoes. In the train, we children stayed in a separate compartment and were not searched for valuables.

Upon arriving at my uncle's home in Neustadt/Holstein (northern part of Germany), we saw a big change in my grandmother's health and mental state. The adjustments for her were difficult, and my grandfather did not make it any easier on her, as he often got violent towards her. At that moment, Grandmother's hopes and expectations started to diminish. Now we lived in a different household, and Grandmother, who was used to caring for our household, lost her tasks. She felt lost and not needed. In addition, we children had been placed in a private school far away and she missed us very much.

Due to the fact that I could not handle and adjust to this private school, I made sure that I was transferred back to Neustadt, the town where my uncle was residing. There I was able to finish my middle school successfully. But the most important issue was that I was close to my grandmother, who became very ill, and who lost her will to live. Her other children did not spend time with her. I was the only one she allowed to be around and feed her. Grandfather came home one day and threatened her again. And then he said, "You will die soon, therefore, you better give me your ruby ring, which I will give as a present to our daughter Maria."

Aunt Maria was their first child, but born out of wedlock. Nobody knew it at that time. It was shameful, and therefore, Aunt Maria was raised by Grandmother's parents in Weselin in the Rhine River area. Due to the distance and circumstances, Grandmother and her daughter did not have a close relationship. This also might have been the reason why Aunt Maria was not willing to invite her mother to her house upon arrival in West Germany. On the other hand, Opa visited his daughter several times, although it was his, as well as Grandmother's fault that they had an illegitimate child.

Grandmother's health required her to be admitted to the local hospital. I was told that she was constantly calling my name during her last night in the hospital before she died.

I was lucky to see her one last time on the day she died. When I tiptoed into the room, her eyes were closed, but she knew I was there. Her last words were, "You are a good and giving soul. Remember, you will hardly receive a thank you from people you have helped. The award will come from an unexpected source." Two hours later she was dead. My Aunt Hanna, who knew how close I was to my grandmother, did not allow me to participate in the visitation at the funeral home. She told me, "You should remember your grandmother as a lively and sincere person."

Now when I think about her it brings tears to my eyes. I visited her grave as often as I could when I was in the area. I still carry memories in my heart and wish that she would have had a better life.

I love you grandmother, wherever you are.

Chapter 6
Love and Sorrow for a Mother

It was Sunday, December 2, 2007, when we received a call from the nursing home in Meerbusch, Germany. We were told that our mother passed away. For four years she had been in full-time care because she was very fragile and suffered from dementia. She was not able to take care of herself. In the last two weeks of her life she caught pneumonia, which led to her death. Even though we were prepared for that, it still was a shock.

It happened that my sister had already scheduled her trip to Germany for quite some time, but the departure date was coincidental. In one way it was fortunate because my sister Karin could handle all the formalities for the cremation and bring the ashes to the States. The funeral ceremony was to be in Illinois. My brother-in-law arranged the ceremony with a Catholic priest in the church as well as at the cemetery. The date was set for the fifteenth of December. I made an airline reservation for the fourteenth from Cincinnati to Chicago. My sister picked me up at O'Hare Airport. Everything turned out perfectly, but a heavy snowstorm kicked in on the day of the funeral. First we participated in the sermon and the burial. After that a family lunch in a restaurant nearby was arranged. We all had a chance to talk and remember our mother and the children their Oma (Grandma). In this chapter I try to explain my feelings towards my mother, which were not always positive.

After my grandmother passed away in 1957, I felt lost and mourned for ten years. I visited the grave on a regular basis, even when I started my education in Hamburg. My aunt Hanna tried to console me and mentioned that Grandmother did not want to have her daughter—my mother—near her bedside. This took me by surprise. Now I understood why she wanted me on her side the last couple of weeks before she died. Often I asked myself the question of what happened between my mother and grandmother. I knew only that my grandmother spoiled her daughter in her youth. But my mother tended to be closer to her father, my grandfather, and she never even mentioned her mom in the later days. She only talked about the parties and banquets that she attended together with her father. For the first time it occurred to me that it wasn't only me whose relationship was estranged with my mother. This feeling deepened more and more when I moved to Hamburg and continued my education.

In 2002, my mother turned eighty-seven. She lived in Germany by herself and did manage to get around well. Her health was pretty good, but her memory was pretty much completely gone. We did not realize how bad it was and did not know when it began. She was a pretty good actress, and knew how to cover it up. There was hardly any communication between her and us children.

Our relationship never seemed to be warm or filled with sincerity. I loved her dearly, though. Over the years, this love turned into sorrow, and yes, I felt bad for her that she was missing so many pleasant moments due to her bitterness and isolation. This started a long time ago, and for years, my sister and I tried to pull down the other's façade. Mother was very secretive. It was very hard for both of us as daughters, who were living in the U.S., to care for her, not knowing how she felt, what she was thinking, and what the real status of her health was. Over the years there were so many lies about her vision. She did not want us to find a good doctor for her. Therefore, we gave up and limited our efforts to frequent phone calls and visits once a year.

In retrospect, specific happenings and memories from my childhood influenced my life, and I never overcame particular occurrences. That's why, even today, unconscious anger surfaces. I was told that I should write down those feelings in order to help me find inner peace. That's why I've dedicated this chapter to my mother.

I admit I was a kind of wild child, spoiled by my grandmother. Danger quite often overshadowed me, so I was not afraid of anything. My older sister Karin was calm, obedient and scared of many things, specifically darkness. An explanation for that might be a shock my mother experienced while she was pregnant with Karin. This might have transferred to the child. Because of that, the family and I had the impression that Mother felt more drawn to my sister as a protector. Karin always received Mother's and Grandfather's attention either in a loving or disciplinary way when she talked back in a less than respectful manner.

In my case, I got the attention from neighbors, who also supplied first aid when I injured myself. This happened very often. I developed a certain independence and stubbornness. Our different temperaments and personalities could have been the reason why Mother treated us differently.

I can't remember that Mother ever put her arms around me or had me sit on her lap. That might have been why I developed opposition. However, many years later in a discussion, Mother admitted it. I assume that I got jealous, felt left out and I tried to fight it. However, intrigues, false statements by my mother, which took place over the years, made it very difficult for me. I had no way to defend my reputation since I was not present at the time those rumors were spread around.

I called my sister "Mamachild" because Mother protected her while she was still young. Mother found excuses for whatever my sister had done, good or bad. I got more and more engaged at school activities and was focused on my studies. Therefore, I was proud to be a better student and of the awards that came with it. At home, however, I heard a constant statement: "Your sister will study languages and be successful."

Well, it never happened. Nevertheless, I developed my personality based on communication with people, involvement in sporting activities, and had the urge to fight against all odds. Call it "Survivor at an early age!"

The years as a teenager were very uneasy. It was the time we had to change the country (Poland in 1955), the language, and the hardest, to leave my very first boyfriend, Janusz. Suddenly our small family was torn apart. Quite often I felt very lonely and wished Mother would be there. I hoped we could talk out and resolve our differences. But Mother was never available, or she chose not to make herself available.

She struggled with jobs, and her ambition to prove herself against all odds made it quite difficult for her as she was forty years old. Certainly, she did not find any support within the family, and her siblings, Uncle Theo and Uncle George, often made fun of her. She felt hurt and distanced herself from the family. It was not easy to learn and be trained for new jobs while also having two teenage girls to care for. She did her best but isolated herself over time.

Suddenly, after sixteen years as a widow, she developed a need to start living and enjoying life. She had missed a lot in her life because of the war and later the occupation of our homeland. A partner was missing in her life. Still, we were in her life and needed her attention, but I did not get much of it. There were sad moments in my life and I wished I would have had a father. In those lonely moments I turned either to a priest or a family doctor for advice and moral support.

Irma Pallas

When my grandmother died in 1958 I was filled with deep sadness, hardship at school and family problems while I finished the school in Neustadt (the town where my uncle's family resided). These drew me back into isolation, sadness and losing the will to live.

My uncle, a very strict and demanding person, took advantage of the situation and abused me mentally for months, and later physically. For ten years we hardly talked to each other, and then, only when the conversation was necessary. I mentioned the situation and experience to my mother, however, she did not want to believe me, or rather ignored it. I knew that she had her own issues towards her brother.

During the summer vacation of 1958, Mother invited me to spend some time in the spa/recreation area, Bad Mergentheim, where she had worked as masseuse. I attended dancing school and met a lot of interesting people. For the first time I enjoyed myself, but at home more and more fights developed. It was obvious that Mother was jealous of me for being relaxed and happy. Again I realized that she was searching for a male partner, which I understood perfectly. She lost her husband, our father, very early. But there were hundreds of women who experienced the same tragedy. Certainly it was not easy to find a partner in the same age range. She started to clinch onto married men, which did not bring much luck, but rather disappointment. Her bitterness got stronger and stronger. She stopped communicating with the family in order to avoid any sensitive questions. When she was asked about the job, her traveling or other private issues, she turned into a nasty and aggressive person.

In 1959 I enrolled in the medical school in Hamburg, while my sister was in Kassel specializing in chemistry. At this time, as I learned later, Mother kept in very close contact with my sister. Mother apparently did not feel a need to bother with me. During the two education years I experienced serious health problems. It was a bladder infection, caused by a rare virus. A friend, who was my very first serious involvement, made sure I got the proper medical attention. I was admitted to the hospital in which I studied chemistry. It was the famous Tropical Institute, which treated patients with tropical illnesses such as malaria.

My mother was informed of my hospitalization and came to visit while I was in the middle of specific tests. Before she entered the hospital room she directed the question: "Is she pregnant?" to the doctor on duty. The nurse happened to hear this and repeated it to me. I broke down in tears. The test had to be interrupted and the doctor gave me some medication so I could rest and compose myself. After that the test could be continued. I was so angry that I refused to see my mother until I turned twenty-one in 1962.

Shortly before my birthday I informed my mother that I would marry a friend whom she resented because he wasn't Catholic, but rather a member of the Masonry. Through a lawyer I requested all the items I had been collecting for my future marriage, such as linen, silver, and jewelry that I had inherited from my grandmother. There were also some gift items which I received on birthdays or other occasions. Later, Mother spread rumors around that I had started court procedures, which never happened. A day before my birthday, Mother and I met at the central train station in Hamburg, since I refused to ask her to my apartment. She handed over a package with my belongings, but only after I had signed an itemized listing.

My marriage did not last longer than five years and was later annulled. My husband was much older than I, and at that time I was grateful for all his help and support.

A separate chapter, Searching for a Father Replacement, will describe all the circumstances.

In the meantime, my sister Karin had accepted a one-year job offer at the University of Chicago and left Germany in 1963. I saw her briefly prior to her departure. Mother accompanied her to the harbor in Bremerhaven where she embarked the vessel Bremen for the journey to the United States. This one year turned into a permanent stay after she met her future husband Guenther-Alan Kogerup. They married in 1964. Mother traveled to the United States for the wedding and also "participated" in their honeymoon. By "participated," I mean that the two lovebirds took an RV—and stayed in it—on their honeymoon. Mother stayed with them in the RV.

Back in Germany, Mother kept up only a limited contact with me. One time I learned that she had to undergo a serious surgery so I rushed to Duesseldorf to be at her side. She always liked to scare us with nonexistent health problems just to get our attention. This surgery, however, was definitely serious. When she awoke from anesthesia, her first question was, "Is Karin here?" She did not say, "I am glad that you are here."

I continued my education by enrolling in evening classes and got involved in English conversation training as well. As a child I had the dream to travel and discover the world. The dream came true at a later time. I was very lucky to find wonderful people whom I called friends and who stood by my side in difficult times. They also opened the door to the world for me.

Beginning in 1971 I started to work for a tourist agency. I was assigned for five months to Moscow and two months to Leningrad, as well as two months on the Greek island of Cyprus. The remaining season time I stayed in Bonn (at that time capital of West Germany). It was very enjoyable and interesting work. With each arriving group of tourists I had mostly good, but sometimes also bad, experiences. The bad experiences were caused by people whom I called "Newly rich" who thought that the lifestyle in Russia was the same as they were used to in the West. They had no idea that those were two different worlds. The Russian people did their best to accommodate tourists, which was not always easy according to the circumstances.

Prior to my leaving for Russia, my mother invited me for dinner. It was December 1970. There was champagne and all kind of goodies, so I got suspicious. This was not the mother I knew, and indeed, after dinner she presented me with an airline ticket to the U.S.

I asked her "Why should I go?" Her answer was, "You should see your sister before you start your job behind the Iron Curtain." I had not seen or spoken to my sister for six years.

Well, I did go, and it turned out to be a very interesting trip. I met my brother-in-law Guenther for the first time, and my two nieces. My brother-in-law observed me very closely. My sister and I had to catch up on all happenings. She showed me pictures and explained what she and Mother used to do together. There were trips to Rome in Italy, Vienna in Austria, and Paris in France. I did not comment on any one of them, but it definitely did hurt very much because I had been left out. Then Karin asked me many questions and made remarks about my life that caught my attention. In reverse, I started to ask her for details and the sources on which some of her statements were based. Finally, I learned what was going on. Rumors and negative stories originated from Mother.

It was time to explain, correct and set the record straight. Nevertheless, Karin tried her best to make me feel comfortable in their house.

Upon my return to Germany, Mother was eager to hear whether I had enjoyed the stay. Again, there was champagne with breakfast. I was not angry. I was very composed when I told her that apparently her bad conscience had forced her to arrange the trip for me.

She looked at me astonished. I told her what I had learned in Karin's house. I asked, "What about the trips you took with Karin?" and "Why did you spread untrue stories about me?"

and "Why did you badmouth me?" There was no answer, just tears, which did not touch or impress me. That wasn't all; similar discussions and arguments followed one year later. I left my mother and hoped that she would come to her senses.

I left for Moscow and settled in the Hotel Intourist. The Russian travel office Intourist was cooperating with the German agency. People in general were very nice and helpful. As soon as I met a tourist from the area where my mother lived, I never missed to pass a letter or gift for her. I wanted her to be involved in my life. When the season ended, I arranged a trip for Mother and me to Moscow, with the chance to go to the Bolshoi Theater and learn about the country behind the Iron Curtain. I paid for the trip, but she stated to the family and my sister that she had to come up with the money. I wish I would have saved the receipt as proof.

My goal was to continue my career based on languages (Polish, English, Russian and French). Two job opportunities opened and I applied first with Lufthansa, the West German airline, for a public relations job, and second with the Office for Foreign Affairs. I had to pass exams for Polish and Russian, and later English. The Office for Foreign Affairs responded a week earlier than Lufthansa. I decided to go with the Foreign Affairs job assignment to Poland. It all happened in January 1972, shortly after Christmas. Since I had finished my tourist guide job in December 1971, I rented a room on a monthly basis until my departure in February.

Bonn, the previous capital of the Federal Republic of Germany, was only one hour away from the town my mother resided in at that time. I informed her about my future job and suggested that we celebrate the Christmas holiday together prior to my leaving. At that time she did not have any plans and agreed. However, one day before Christmas Eve, while I was out of the office visiting the Russian Embassy to obtain visas for our tourists, Mother left a message for me asking me to return her call.

At that point I knew that something was cooking. I was right. During our telephone conversation, Mother stated that she just had a heart attack and preferred to visit my uncle, the surgeon, instead of celebrating with me. Did I believe that? Not really. Too many times Mother played games with us. But still I thought if it really was true, then I had to forgive her. So I drove to her house after work. It was a messy, rainy day, and I had to concentrate on my driving. I was hungry and felt sick in my stomach because I had not eaten even lunch.

Upon arrival in Merbusch, where she was living, I rang the doorbell. Mother opened with a big smile on her face. Nothing indicated that she was not feeling well. At that point my composure left me and I could not control my anger. I started to scream and yell at her: "How dare you scare me for nothing!" I continued:

"This could be our last Christmas ever and you don't even consider or think what I will do on this holiday while you visit your brother."

Because of my suspicion I had already contacted my uncle George in Frankfurt and told him what had happened. He did not hesitate to invite me to his house and spend the holidays with him and my aunt Ingeborg. I did not mention anything to my mother. She probably realized then what she had done to me.

She started to cry and responded: "I can cancel my visit."

"No" I said. "You just go ahead with your plans. You have never cared about me anyway."

The exchange got louder and louder and very nasty. Then she said, "You never gave me grandchildren," and, "You are like your father who always wanted to be the center of attention."

I could only answer, "Didn't you love my father who also was your husband?" and, "Knowing my health situation about having children you should be ashamed even to mention something like that!"

I was expecting an apology, but that never came. In the meantime, it was late and I just wanted to leave. But Mother did not let me go home; she was afraid that on the way something would happen to me. I was too geared up and upset. So I stayed overnight, and when I left the next day I did not see her for quite some time. I got only a message from my aunt Hanna in Neustadt that during this particular Christmas Mother did not talk much and never mentioned a word about what happened between us.

In February of 1974 I was transferred from Warsaw to the Consulate General in Chicago, and in July 1974 I married Stanley Pisz.

In 1976 my mother visited my sister and so I saw her again. We took her on a trip to Canada. She visited the U.S. a dozen times. On purpose I kept her visits in my house very short in order to avoid any friction. One unpleasant visit at my sister's house was when my niece Ingrid got married, and a verbal fight got out of hand. That was why my brother-in-law, who always supported Mother, made sure that she left earlier than planned. The hot discussions were about her bad vision and were based on the video I took at the wedding. When viewing it, Mother insisted that she was not in it. She indeed was shown sitting in the first church row. Suddenly we knew that she was not supposed to drive her car anymore. She was always lying to us, which was scary.

The very last time I saw my mother in the States was on my sister's sixtieth birthday. My brother-in-law thought it would be a surprise for Mom to attend this celebration. Here we all realized that her memory was declining, and still we did not take it too seriously. But strange things happened. My niece picked her up from O'Hare Airport. Mother insisted that she had left a shopping bag with her shoes on the airplane. The plane was searched and nothing was found. Then later at my sister's home she stated that money was lost. She was talking about seven thousand dollars! Later we learned that this

Ordinary Woman

was not true either. She even accused my niece Ingrid about the loss.

In July 2003 we got a call that Mother had fallen and had been admitted to the hospital. She was hurt and needed surgery. We still don't know the reason for her fall in her apartment. She could not remember anything. First my sister Karin flew to Germany, and my husband and I followed twice. Our second trip indicated that mother would never return to her own home. She needed help and supervision. Therefore, my husband and I had to vacate her apartment. It was hard work because we had only four days to sort, clean and discharge many items. We had some help from Mother's friend who managed to get us a container for a few hours. Clothes were given away to people who appreciated them. Paperwork had to be shredded or filed in particular folders. I also found documents for which I had been searching over the years when I worked on family traces. Among them I found two diaries kept by my father six months before he was killed during the war in 1942. Mother never told us about it or ever spoke about him. She had probably cut off those memories long, long time ago.

Following the surgery and recovery time, Mother was admitted to a nursing home. At the beginning she thought it would be temporary, but in time she realized that it was permanent. She had lost her memory.

On July 2005, Mother turned ninety. As a surprise, my sister, I and our husbands scheduled a trip to Germany. A friend of ours from Hamburg joined us as well. The nurses prepared and decorated a room for the celebration. There was enough cake and champagne which she always liked. It was sad to see that she did not recognize the family and friends.

At the table, Karin sat on Mother's left side, and I on her right side. Mother was holding my hand, and when she needed to step out she turned to me and I accompanied her to the bathroom. It made Karin sad that Mother did not call her by name. I think she forgot, and at that point I knew that inside my heart I had made peace with her. The following year we visited her. When I embraced her she started to cry. That was a sign that she recognized me. I called the nursing home frequently to follow up on her health. In December 2006 we learned that Mother had lost her eyesight completely and needed full-time assistance. Our next trip was in May 2007. Each time we went there we thought it would be the last time we would see her alive. We prayed that God would relieve her from that kind of life. She died December 2, 2007. I knew that she would take many secrets to her grave. God bless her.

On Memorial Day in 2008, the whole family gathered together when the tombstone was set on the gravesite in Illinois.

She now may rest in peace.

Chapter 7
The Father I Never Knew

In 2003, my mother had an accident which resulted in surgery, hospitalization, rehabilitation, and finally admission to a nursing home. My sister, my husband and I had to vacate her apartment, which we did step by step. It took us days. We had to sort out clothing and household items.

But more important and interesting were documents, photos and very personal items we found.

Suddenly, we discovered what we never knew: that mother was a very secretive person. She did not include us in her life, and she never talked about our father, her husband. There were many occasions when we mentioned our father and asked questions about him, but those questions were never answered.

I remember the time when I was in a boarding school and was a rebellious student who searched for answers. I felt very lonely. My sister, who was in the same school but in a higher level, was not allowed to help or comfort me. Seminars were scheduled by Jesuit priests who taught and lectured students and prepared us for the outside world. I asked one of the priests for a meeting, since I was desperate to share my thoughts and feelings.

"What is the reason for this session?" the priest asked me.

"Well I feel very lonely, and I don't have a good relationship with my mother, and I am missing my father," I told him.

"What makes you feel like that?" he asked.

"I see parents coming to visit my fellow students, take them home for holidays, but my mother hardly shows up, and if she is comes, we fight."

"What about your father?" the priest asked.

"The only thing I know is that he lost his life on the Eastern Front in 1942." The priest and I prayed together, which gave me some comfort.

Many years went by, and the subject was not touched until I was deployed to Warsaw to work at the German Embassy as a bilingual secretary.

The employed personnel consisted of the locals and dispatched employees from Germany. Among the local co-workers, I met Mrs. Rhode. She was of German descent, and we became friends. To my surprise, she mentioned my late father, and I was very interested in hearing what she knew.

"Your father, as well as my late husband, used to work for the German Police Law Enforcement. Their duties were to protect borders and protect districts in the Czech Republic. Your father was a very handsome man, and was very particular. He was very much liked, and women turned their heads," she told me. Her description of my father made me happy to have at least heard something about him.

In 1972, just before Christmas, I took a few days off to go to Germany and visit my mother. I could hardly wait to tell her the news I learned about my father, and I hoped to hear more from her. It seemed like a puzzle that I wanted so badly to put together, but I was disappointed. My mother was furious, screamed at me and shouted:

"Why do you tell me that? Why don't they let my husband rest in peace?"

I did not understand her state of mind. Rage and jealousy seemed to overcome her at this point and she attacked me verbally:

Ordinary Woman

"You have the same personality as he had. You want to be the center of attention. You don't care about me!"

At this moment I was speechless. The only answer I could give was a question I directed to her:

"Didn't you love my father? You should be proud about the compliments people express. By the way, I do not need to be the center of attention, as you think. Being friendly, helpful and communicative with others results in being surrounded automatically, and you never feel alone."

I think my mother never understood this. Later, I learned a bit more and tried to understand her bitterness.

As I mentioned before, while my sister and I cleaned Mother's apartment, we found two diaries that had been left by my father. Mother had never mentioned anything about them. They would have been helpful at one time when I tried to put our family history together. I had needed documents such as birth certificates, death certificates, and marriage certificates. I had to request those from different courts.

It made me angry when I found all the originals among Mother's correspondence and other documents. But the biggest surprise was when I found photo albums and two diaries. The diaries were handwritten, partially in the old "siterlin" (gothic kind of handwriting), and it took me quite some time to read and type them on a computer. The entries started on January 6, 1942, while my father was stationed in Bruenn in the Czech Republic. The first lines translate as follows:

"These lines are my own thoughts about my lovely wife and mother of my children who once in a while visit me during vacation. She is also able to keep up a family life. The lines are only for you, my dearest Luzie. In case a third party will read these lines so one might know that the first page is explanatory enough."

My father made an entry every day. He described his daily activities, his personal thoughts and his dreams. I realized how much he must have loved his wife and us children. It was war time, and he was confined to a station far away from his family. He made friends with some of the police captains with whom he spent his free time. They went to movies, concerts or to the casino restaurant. They loved to play cards and enjoyed a good glass of wine. But each evening, no matter how late it was, he always made an entry in the diary. For example, he entered: "good night girls, I love you and I miss you."

His duties were not always pleasant. Each day brought him new surprises; he had to check on injured soldiers and bring them home or to a safe place; he visited camps in order to interview, or investigate prisoners, and check their cases. He had to accompany the major of his battalion to various places and meetings. Most of the time when he tried to schedule a vacation, the request was denied with no explanation given. His superior was an unfriendly and sometimes nasty person. It made my father angry and sad. Therefore, his only hope was to receive almost every day a letter from his wife. But that was not the case. Father seemed to forget that she was occupied raising his children. My sister had turned just two, and I was eleven months old. Small children needed a lot of attention and filled Mother's daily schedule completely.

My father was the happiest when a letter or a parcel arrived. That was a reason to celebrate with his companions.

There were moments when he was filled with melancholy and asked himself the question: "How can we describe our marriage? To which group of couples do we belong? We are separated and each of us has a different kind of life. You are in Hindenburg and I am in Bruin. We both wait desperately for a vacation time in order to be together. To wait is our daily problem. To complain does not help, we can only hope."

In another entry he showed concern for his family in case he died. His thoughts were to make sure that his wife would be safe and have a secure life. He wrote, "So many people die daily, and I might too. How can my wife survive and continue? I don't want to die, but nevertheless, I have to think about it. I feel responsible for the future of my family."

In another entry he expressed fear that he might be sent to the battlefield on the Eastern Front. He said, "I have to go, but not as a soldier. Our police battalion should stay here for security reasons, apparently they need us as a backup. We have to obey the orders." He wrote further:

"I have one more wish: to see you and tell you how much I love you. I want to embrace you, feel your heartbeat. I want to take my children Karin and Irmgard in my arms and kiss them. Karin should whisper in my ears 'Daddy,' and Irmgard should smile at me. This I would like to take with me in my memory. I also know that it will break your heart to see me go. I always hear your words, 'Darling come back soon.'"

Meanwhile, my father was reassigned from Bruin to Radom, Zamosc and Lublin in central Poland. He did not like it at all. The environment was poorly kept and camps and cemeteries were in terrible shape. It made everyone sick to their stomachs.

The second diary describes the time in Lublin, his work, meetings, and worries. Every day, different orders were received and then overruled. Nobody really knew what the next news would bring. His comrades were promoted and sent to different places. My father's promotion was always withheld because his superior managed to do so. Nobody ever understood this.

On April 24, 1942, he wrote:

"Today is our anniversary. Six years ago we married, and due to this occasion I tried to write down my thoughts and observations. I experienced a lot of luck being close to you. Now that the order came to leave for the east front within the next twenty-four hours, this will be my last entry. One of my comrades will see you and bring my diaries. Please continue with your entries. I trust and count that this message will not discourage you. Please inform my mother that I left Lublin.

Goodbye my dearest and trustful wife. I remain forever your husband, Willy."

My mother continued the entries starting May 7, 1942, until June 15, 1942. On that day a letter came announcing the sad news that my father had been killed in action. Not knowing what had happened on June 6, 1942, she wrote:

"Today, my night was terrible. My arms were numb. I could not sleep. Are my nerves so sick or what is it? Are you well, my Willy? I worry about you. I write to you daily and hope you receive my mail. The children are doing well. Our thoughts are with you, Daddy."

The letter that came on June 15, 1942, was signed by Major Knifflin. He confirmed that on June 6, my father had been hit by shellfire. It was a fatal hit. On reading the Major's letter, my mother broke down and cried out loud calling: "Willy!" As mentioned before, Mother never talked about our dad. We do not know whether it was bitterness or if she wanted to forget and wipe out the memory.

Today, Mother is dead. She was four years in a poor state of mind in a nursing home. During my visits I still tried to ask her about my father and even mentioned his name, Willy. At that moment she started to talk about my grandfather. There was nothing left in her memory about my father.

Years ago while my aunt Gertrud (father's sister) was still alive, she told me how much she adored her brother and how much she missed him. He was always a gentleman, elegant and liked to entertain.

I wish he will rest in peace as well, and oh, how much I would have loved to have had him around.

Chapter 8
Relationships a Life Experience

How do we know the difference between relationships we are supposed to pursue and ones we are supposed to avoid? The answers are not easy, and they take work, patience and a lot of self-honesty. They can bring joy or pain just thinking about them. It seems to be so long ago when I experienced both kinds of relationships. Here is one on sexual education and that's also filled with deep emotion and friendship.

Reports about teenage pregnancy, college rapes, assaults and traumatic experience are not new to us anymore. Times have changed drastically. These days, everything is so open because of television and other media sources. Talk show psychiatrists try to explain and educate not only the victims, but especially parents who might have missed finding the time and courage to talk to their children about sex. Children do not have the ability to foresee consequences resulting from a flirt or show-off-play, or even an unexpected assault.

In the time I grew up these subjects were not discussed. Never. But again, back then we did not hear about rapes, Aids, HIV and other threatening diseases. I learned to be an informed teenager after a while.

My mother, as a single parent, had a busy life herself, not only work-wise, but also in searching for a partner who could share the load of parenting. Because she had not been educated about sex in her young years, she never considered talking about it with her children. My sister Karin and I had to educate ourselves with life experiences.

I remember my first relationship very well. A "late bloomer" (in 1958) one would describe me. I was seventeen years old. Friends and schoolmates had experienced their sex education already at earlier age. I spent my vacation that year in a spa area in southern Germany where my mother worked. It was in Bad Mergentheim, one of the rehabilitation and health resorts. All towns with the name starting as "Bad" are considered health resorts. Post operation therapies were applied to patients in order to improve the healing process. In Germany, those treatments were covered by health insurance, but today, the benefits have been cut and patients need to carry about fifty percent of the cost. Treatments are prescribed by the treating doctors, and often an insurance doctor has to confirm the treatment needs.

Bad Mergentheim is located in southern Germany along the River Tauber. Therefore, people talk about the Tauber-Tal, which translates to Tauber Valley. This valley is marked with the blooming meadows and the sun-spoiled wine landscape.

One of the nicest Kurparks, or Revitalization Parks, is located in Bad Mergentheim. Secluded and comfortable pedestrian alleys allow patients to walk through the park, and meet and get acquainted with others while slowly drinking the warm and healing spring waters. Patients were treated in medical facilities called sanatoriums. There had been many of those facilities around the town, and many offered lodging. Depending on the treatment schedules, the rest of the days were for socializing. It was known that people met, accompanied each other and even started affairs.

I had spent already once my vacation in Bad Mergentheim, and at that time my sister joined me. My mother, who was working as a masseuse therapist in one of those sanatoriums, arranged for us to take dancing lessons at a dancing school.

We both enjoyed it and we had very talented dancing partners. I only remember the name of my partner, Klaus.

Because we were excellent dancers, the teacher used us for show-dancing. It was fun, but we did not keep in touch with our partners when we left.

A year later, I visited my mother by myself and thought that we could solve our existing differences. I was wrong. My mom was bitter because of her disappointments in life, and she developed a jealousy towards me. She did not approve my communication skills or of my ability to meet people.

I met Siegfried, a perfect gentleman fifteen years my senior, in a cafe while I enjoyed a casual Ice coffee (coffee with vanilla ice cream and topped with whipped cream). I suddenly heard a voice from the neighbor's table:

"Since it appears you are alone, would you like to join me?"

I turned around, smiled and replied, "With pleasure."

I needed someone to talk to because of the estranged relationship with my mother. Siegfried and I seemed to like each other, and we had an open dialogue.

We met every day of his remaining stay. We walked through the park and attended afternoon concerts. One day he arranged a picnic in a secluded field area. Due to the fact that I had not yet experienced an intimate relationship, I thought, "It might as well be now. Some day it has to start anyway." We talked about it and touched on the subject.

As I recall, I asked him a lot of questions about intimacy and sex. The questions I asked were probably silly, but Siegfried did not mind. He answered and explained in detail as a parent or teacher would have. There were no "birds and bees" stories. I remember the unusual questions such as, "When should a girl have her first sex experience?" or, "Explain the feelings," and, "When and how does a woman or girl loses her virginity?"

Siegfried answered the questions seriously and without any jokes. He also mentioned that a good first experience should be memorized for life. Later, our encounter started with a kiss, and for the very first time, I experienced the most intimate and lovely moments which a woman can expect. I considered it an education that helped me to handle and understand difficult situations in which I was confronted at a later time. I started to think about whether men who made advances towards me were jerks or macho men who had problems with their sex lives. Those people freaked me out, and I ignored them completely.

Following an abusive marriage, I lost my confidence in being a gentle love maker. I rather would say that I was scared to get involved. On the other side, I concentrated on my work.

For many years I knew Wolfgang and his wife, whom I had met many years prior. Wolfgang was a radio amateur and had contact with my brother-in-law Alan in the U.S., and another German friend, Heinz. I did not know much about him, and my brother-in-law later described him as a womanizer. But there was a reason for giving a bad opinion about another person. There must have been some differences in the past between Wolfgang and Alan which originated from the time Alan was a member of the U.S. Army. I never learned about the details and was not interested in them.

When I returned to Hamburg for a short time, I made a courtesy visit to the shop. He specialized in radio and phone installations in cars. Wolfgang just was building up. We talked and he told me that his wife had just left him for an "around the world" trip on a trade vessel. She was restless and had the need to do so. Wolfgang had a hard time dealing with it and had to care for his teenage son Carsten, as well as for the business. He said, "I feel to be chained and imprisoned." As I learned later, his wife came back, but shortly after that she died of heart failure. Time went by, and in 1971, I was already in Moscow and came back few times to Hamburg.

Ordinary Woman

Since Wolfgang and I stayed in contact, he asked me to visit while I was on the way to my family in Neustadt. Wolfgang resided half-way from Hamburg to Neustadt. I accepted the invitation. He had a beautifully and tastefully decorated home, which made everyone feel welcome. In one way, Wolfgang seemed to be shy, but again, he was a perfect host. I liked him very much, and after a while I had no objections to starting an intimate relationship with him. He was very gentle, and never forced himself on me. There was wine, candlelight and soft music, which gave a cozy feeling. We talked, made love and had a lot of fun whenever we met later on. I introduced him to my family in Neustadt. We did not make any commitment to each other. For me, it was a wonderful friendship. Wolfgang was honest with me when he said, "I feel free after all the family troubles, and therefore I am seeing a lot of woman, but you were the best in my life."

The last time I talked to him on the phone from the U.S. was in 2009. At that time he had a nurse in his house around the clock. He was very sick. The last message I received from my brother-in-law was that Wolfgang had passed away at the age of eighty-one.

Part Two
The Rough Road Ahead

Chapter 9
Hamburg – My Second Home

In August, 1959, I enrolled into medical school at the biggest hospital in Hamburg, St. Georg. I had decided to become a Medical Technical Assistant, and later I studied clinical chemistry at the medical centers and hospitals. It was a two-year program that consisted of one year of theory and one year of practice in different hospital departments and labs. Being away from my family was not always easy, but this city embraced me in all ways.

In order to introduce the city to the reader, I informed myself about its history and found the following:

"After the discovery of America and the sea route to Asia, as from 1550, Hamburg became one of the most important ports of entry in Europe. With the increase in shipping and world trade in the second half of the 19th century, Hamburg had to further expand its port and storage capacities. The construction of the Speicherstadt, or storage city district, (1881-1888) was the first step in this direction. In the decades that followed, the port was expanded to the opposite shore of the Elbe River.

"The creation of the free port (1888) made Hamburg one the world's biggest warehouse locations for coffee, cocoa, spices and carpets. The construction of the Kiel Canal (1895) further increased the port's attractiveness, as a direct and fast link to the Baltic Sea area was now guaranteed. It was now the member of the HANSA. This name was indicating and involving all Baltic-Sea Port-Cities which were involved into sea way trade market. Other cities such as Lübeck, Bremen, Rostock and Stralsund were HANSA members as well."

When I came to Hamburg, I learned that there were thirty theatres, six music halls, ten cabarets and fifty state and private museums. Further, there were four thousand restaurants, of which two thousand four hundred offered foreign cuisine. As the years went by, only one or two cabarets remained, and only one of the big theaters survived the ups and down of the economy.

Together with friends I loved to stroll at the banks of the Elbe River and the Alster. Often on weekends it drew me to the port. Over the speaker, vessels were greeted in their native languages when they approached the harbor. The view was impressive and it offered a special perspective on the panorama of Hamburg.

The time in Hamburg (about twelve years) taught me to adjust to city life. As a student with little money available, it was important to for me to search for a room, which families advertised for renting. In such cases, I had to share a bathroom and kitchen and had to observe the rules that had been set. Several times in those twelve years, I changed living locations because of where my jobs were located.

The people in northern Germany are very distant, businesslike, but also honest. It took me five years to build up contacts and establish friendships that have lasted forever. I was once invited to a dinner-dance in the Hotel Atlantic that was organized by publishing houses. I danced to the music of James Last. Friends gave a toast saying, "Now you have been accepted to the Hamburg Society." I felt honored.

Life was not always easy. I was still very young, and I experienced good and bad times. However, I had to make choices to whom to turn to when I needed support and help. My family was not available, therefore, I had to rely on my few friends who were there during those dark moments.

Those few close friends were Robert Beck, Hannelore Duering and Dr. Neumann. My mother did not have money to support me; she was just able to pay for the education, the monthly rent and allowance, which didn't cover my other expenses. Therefore, I was glad when the doorbell would ring and a friend like Robert Beck invited me for a proper meal. Ingrid, one of my roommates once said, "You are either on top or emotionally down. Sometimes you do not know how to get through the month." She was right. There was never a middle stage in my life.

That's also why I worked on the weekends in the publishing house. I packed and loaded magazines for the next day's deliveries. It involved a lot of heavy lifting, which caused me spine problems. For many years I had to be treated to ease the pain. After a while, I had to give this work up. I learned about blood donation within our medical institute and donated six times. I was paid thirty Deutschmarks and I got a proper breakfast. It was also the time when I had to do my class assignments for my radiology and photography classes. Most of the time I was in the darkroom. This was too much for my body. I became anemic and weak and could not continue donating blood.

When I finished my education, I started a job at a doctor's office. It was Dr. Neumann who employed me as a medical assistant, and I loved this job. The relationship with the patients, and especially with children, was outstanding. Dr. Neumann helped me in moments of despair. With my first salaries I finally found an apartment and covered the expenses.

One of the patients was Hannelore Duering, whom I saw frequently and who came with her daughter Christina. We got acquainted, and I was invited to her home several times. When Hannelore's marriage fell apart, I took Christina into my house and was her foster mom for a short period of time. She called me Aunt Irma, and still does today, even though she's more than fifty years old. We remained in close contact for years. In 2007, we visited Hamburg and we made sure to see Hannelore, as well as Christina. Even though many years had passed, it seemed like we had never parted.

The banks of the Elbe and the Alster Rivers are perfect for a stroll. Especially the River Alster, which starts as a lake in the center of the city and connects with channels. It's an attraction for tourists to take on sightseeing boat tours through and around the city. In the heart of the city, the River Alster is surrounded by cafes, exclusive hotels and parks. The area is very delightful. This was my favorite destination to go shopping or relax in a street cafe. It was easy for me to move around with the underground trains and buses for a small fare. My favorite shopping area was on Neuer Wall and Jungfernstieg streets. There were department stores, but more appealing were the boutiques. There I bought my hats, which helped to lift my spirit in dark moments. Thankfully, I never experienced depression. As a matter of fact, I did not have this word in my vocabulary. Unfortunately, the hat-fashion is not in anymore.

One of the less positive experiences in Hamburg was when I got sick and was admitted to the Tropical Institute. The doctors could not define the cause of my bladder infection. This was the time during my medical education when I was involved in the chemistry practice. The four weeks during which I was treated were educational.

The Tropical Institute was located in the area overlooking Hamburg Harbor. This hospital specialized in treatments originating from tropical climates such as malaria and other blood diseases. It was also mentioned that in this area Eros Centers opened and the famous Herbert Strasse, known as Prostitute Alley, was not far away. Those "ladies" had to show up at the labs frequently for blood tests.

Ordinary Woman

The work in the laboratory was interesting and challenging. Finally, our professor of bacteriology helped find the cause of my infection. In the lab we started cultures using probes of blood and urine. Under the microscope we discovered the coli-bacteria which caused the infection in my bladder. This helped to find the proper medication and I recovered fairly quickly.

The area around Hamburg is especially delightful. The fruit-growing area of the Altes Land (Old Land), with its old farm houses, is especially suited for excursions by bus or on bicycle. The historic old towns of Stade and Luneburg can be reached in half an hour. I had spent a one-week vacation in this area, which was really relaxing. In the summer I took the train from Hamburg to Luebeck, or to the beach on the Baltic Sea. My family resided at that time north of Luebeck, in Neustadt, and it took ninety minutes by car to get there.

In 1962, heavy rains caused the levees of the river Elbe to burst and flooded the lower Altes Land. The center of Hamburg was under water as well, along with the city hall's (Rathaus) basement. Its famous restaurant and winery were destroyed, and one hundred and sixty lives were lost. It was a tragic experience that taught people to improve the levees. Luckily, I was living on the opposite side of the town, and consequently, was not in danger. The climate in Hamburg is known as breezy and wet. "If it rains it pours," is the saying there. Only a monument remains as a memorial to the flood and lost lives.

Since I did not see any advancement in the medical job, I began to attend night school, where I studied shorthand, typing, and general office work. In addition, I took a semester of English. This helped me later to change my occupation from medical work to office administration, and later I turned my attention to the travel business. That's why I left Hamburg. Whenever my husband and I are in Germany, we do not miss a visit to this wonderful city which gives me the feeling of being home again.

Chapter 10
Searching for a Father Replacement

There were moments in life that were filled with struggle, such as school or work, missing support, and family love. Emptiness led me to act in the strangest ways, either to fight for acceptance or to give up. Here is an example out of my life.

In 1960, in Hamburg a relationship started. At that time I still attended a medical school and struggled with my studies as well as my health, and I was ready to give up. Due to the fact that money was short, I shared a room with a girlfriend who tried very hard to support me psychologically.

My mother was far away and we hardly kept in touch. I knew that she was not able to give my sister (in a different town and school) and me a better monetary allowance. Therefore, I decided either to donate blood for a breakfast and money, and additionally, to work on weekends at a publishing house. It was hard work packing and lifting packages in the shipping department. This affected my health very much, specifically my spine. After a while, I was close to collapse.

To get home from school I had to take the subway train. The distance to the station was a fifteen-minute walk. To get to the main train station I had to take the street known as Pick-up Alley. In the afternoons or evenings, ladies/girls were picked up by businessmen.

My mood swings were pretty bad, and I thought that the final solution would be to sell myself on the streets. At that point I didn't care anymore what would happen to me. On the way to the central station I passed the street where I planned to try my luck at prostitution, but was rescued by a man who ended up being my first husband. The future, however, taught me that marrying him was a bad decision. While I was walking there, a car stopped, the window opened and I heard a question directed to me.

"Can I help you? Do you need a ride?" the man said to me. I was startled for a moment but accepted. I did not care anymore. The man introduced himself:

"My name is Karl-Heinz B. and I am just passing by. Watching you I thought you needed some help."

"Yes, indeed you are right. I just don't feel well," I answered.

I thanked him. He gave me a ride home. On the way he asked me:

"When was the last time you had a good meal?"

This question brought me back to reality. I honestly did not remember. The only thing I had eaten was yoghurt and some fruits.

The man, Karl-Heinz Bettels, told me that he was still married, and added:

"But I am separated from my wife. We are estranged."

A friendship started, and he supported me with my studies, and encouraged me to take additional business classes in the evening. After a while he offered me part-time work in his office. This friendly relationship lasted until he divorced his wife.

Meanwhile, I worked full time at a doctor's office, and afterwards in Karl-Heinz's engineering office. During evening classes I learned secretary skills as well as bookkeeping. After a full year working at the doctor's office I terminated my job. I started to work for Karl- Heinz. He was a very demanding employer. True, I learned a lot and improved my business skills, however, I hardly got paid and the hours were long.

On my twenty-first birthday we were married. My family did not approve of this relationship for several reasons. Karl-Heinz did not have any religious beliefs, while I was raised Catholic. My family did not believe in divorce, but Karl-Heinz was divorced. The last, but most important reason was that Karl-Heinz was an active member of the Freemasons. My family was strongly involved with the Catholic Church, and the church had its own opinion about the Freemasons. My grandfather opposed Freemasons, and he wrote me a letter that stated, "You signed a blood pact with the devil," and, "This is what the Freemasons practice." Such letters continued for a while. Finally, I did not accept any mail from my family, which resulted in no communication with them for the next three years. The situation made me so angry that I even did not allow my mother to enter our apartment.

As my husband, Karl-Heinz, changed drastically. The pressure with his business, shortage of money, alimony payments for his son Carsten (eight years old at that time) turned him into a very tempered and abusive man. He would check my typed letters against the light in order to see if I had made any corrections. Computers did not exist at that time, and if he discovered one mistake, the letter had to be retyped no matter how late it was.

Jealousy started to develop while I accompanied him to machine tool shows in Hannover. He did not like it when show visitors or suppliers paid attention to me. He controlled my life step by step.

It got worse when he complained that my body was not sexy enough. He bought a massage unit for breast enlargement and other cosmetic appliances. The best way to describe him was that he was sex-driven. When he whistled, I had to be ready for the bedroom no matter what time of the day or night it was, or whether I was tired or sick. There were no excuses. I had to obey.

Years went by which were torture for me because if I refused to have sex with him he would rage. His rage was indescribable. He would throw me on the bed and force himself on me. He raped me several times. My search for a father replacement was so wrong. Thinking and hoping that in him I would find a supportive and loving person was crazy.

At the age of twenty-five I was aged beyond my years, and neighbors and friends started to worry about me.

After four years of marriage, I finally found the courage to ask for divorce. I took few days off and went to a spa area just to clear my mind and relax. Karl-Heinz knew where to reach me. I did not have any secrets. I wanted him to think about the situation and our future. This request was so unexpected to him. Suddenly he realized how serious I was. Karl-Heinz came to the spa area, picked me up. He cried, fell on his knees and begged not to leave him. He even took me on a flight to Berlin as reconciliation. During this flight I got sick. This sickness turned out to be pregnancy. I told him of that upon our return, and he became furious. He forced me to have an abortion. Since abortions were illegal, I needed to find a doctor who would perform it. I was told that the only solution would be to go to England. This was out of the question. Finally I found a doctor. I needed money to pay for it, but my husband would not give it to me. His statement was:

"You brought yourself into this situation now you find a way out." He punished me by pressing burning cigarette butts on my breasts and arms, and did this even in front of others. In desperation, I secretly contacted some friends who helped me with money. They gave me the money under one condition: that I would divorce my husband. That I promised.

Finally I found the courage to move out. While he was gone I packed two suitcases and walked out. I found a secluded place to stay with another family. It was then that the heavy weight on me seemed to subside. I knew that he found a lady companion as revenge.

I stayed with the family for a while and searched for a job as business administrator. First I found part-time jobs, and later, a full-time job at a trading company in downtown Hamburg.

Karl-Heinz finally realized that this was not a game. I filed for divorce, and few months later the divorce procedures started. It did not take long for the judge to announce the verdict. I still hear his words:

"Mr. Bettels, one day you will be sorry that you lost a person who helped you through bad times and whom you treated inhumanely." With these words he ended the court session. Karl-Heinz had to pay back the amount I inherited from my grandfather and invested into his company. Later our marriage was annulled.

Many years passed before my friends in Hamburg told me that Karl-Heinz had been married six times. Twice he brought African women to the country, married them, and treated them as slaves. The last message I got in 1992 was that he was living on welfare and in very poor health..

It is important to me to mention that there was a person who was particularly close to me, a friend of a distant family who deserves my sincere thanks. Robert stood by my side like a guardian angel. He appeared when I was in desperate need of an ear and friendship. I remember the time when I was still in school and didn't have money to live through the month, nor food. Suddenly there would be a knock on the door, and there would be Robert, asking me to accompany him to dinner. It was always a relief seeing him, talking to him and feeling secure. He also gave me money to cover abortion expenses while I was still married to Karl-Heinz. Our friendship lasted for years until I took a job for a travel office, and later for the Ministry of Foreign Affairs.

I missed Robert very much, but my life continued in positive way and I established myself for the future.

Chapter 11
Romance with a Show off Person

"How do I meet or find a good partner?" That's what I asked myself. I did not want to do something which seemed to improper at that time, so I decided to answer an ad which I found in some tabloids. One of those ads intrigued me. And here came Horst R. into the picture. It happened in Hamburg.

Horst was just divorced and starting a new life. I met him in a cafe, and later we started dating. He was handsome, very successful and athletic. He played tennis, and during the winter season, he regularly went to Davos, Switzerland, to ski. He enjoyed being among the established people. At home, everything was fine and dandy as long he did not have to pay for his girlfriend. He never invited me to join him on his trips. Even his sister, Margot, whom he loved dearly and who lived in Munich, used to pay for her own dinner if we went out to a restaurant.

It was true that I did not have money to pay for sports equipment and extravagant trips. I was too poor for him to be seen with me. It certainly did hurt because I expected a little more understanding and support. Mostly, I missed the cultural life. There was no music or theater that could interest him. It might sound idiotic, but I actually thought for a while about whether to continue this relationship, which was neither exciting nor fulfilling. Nevertheless, I developed deep feelings for him, which unfortunately, were not reciprocated.

Horst owned a condominium that was very beautiful and tastefully decorated with drapes, wallpaper, lamps and paintings on the walls. It was a picture of harmony. He was financially well situated and drove only upscale BMWs. He knew how to represent his business position, as well as himself personally. Finally, it dawned on me that there was no future with him and that I was wasting my time.

Changes in my employment, such as relocation, helped me to make the decision. We parted as friends, and later we met once or twice at his sister's home in Munich. Margot was a lovely and warm-hearted lady who was not always blessed with luck.

Her first marriage ended after the birth of her son; her second husband was abusive, mentally and physically. It got worse when Margot discovered that her teenage son had turned into a druggy and had disappeared. She just could not believe and accept the truth.

She had no support or comfort from her brother's side, nor from her husband, who then left her for good.

While I visited, her she begged me twice to accompany her in searching for her son. We walked from one pub to another where we assumed he could be found. Margot carried a little shopping bag with her containing clean underwear for her son. When we finally spotted him, Margot broke down crying. The environment was dirty, full of smoke, young people staring blankly into space and a pregnant girl who was almost unconscious. Margot's son, Ulf, refused to come home.

The next day we contacted social workers, in the hope of getting some help with rescuing Ulf. The answer was, "As long as the drug-using person does not ask for help by himself, we cannot do anything. It is against the law to force a person to get treatments."

Horst hated his nephew and did not show any tolerance for him, and never offered him advice or help. This was the last time I saw Horst for a while. But there is a saying, "You always meet twice in your life." That happened in 2001.

After twenty years, when I visited Germany with my husband, we passed through Munich and visited my girlfriend Rita, a doctor of internal medicine. I had the urge to find out whether Margot was still listed in the phone book under the same address. Looking through the phone book I discovered that she indeed was listed. I called her immediately. She was home and recognized my voice and was excited and touched that I remembered her. I knew that several years prior, she had been treated for breast cancer and was now a survivor.

"I am okay now," she assured me. Then she said, "Please call Horst. He lives fifty kilometers away from Hamburg. He never married after you left him, but he lives with a lady (Karin) for fifteen years now."

Margot gave me the address and phone number, and I called him. Horst was home and answered the phone. He also recognized my voice and could not believe that I was visiting Munich. We talked for a while and he invited us to visit him at the next available chance, which we accepted.

On the way back to Hamburg we visited him. Karin, his girlfriend, was a very nice hostess and she made us welcome. The meeting was very pleasant. We hugged each other and talked about our life in the U.S. Common subjects were exchanged between Horst and my husband Rudi, who is an engineer as well.

Horst told me that he was not in good health.

"Twice I had a heart attack and ended up in the hospital," He said. "Recently I was diagnosed with diabetes. In addition, I have a slipped disc, which makes certain movements impossible."

He told us about some trips he had taken to South Africa, but said he could not travel anymore on his own. It was necessary that he had someone around to care for him. Still, he had the desire to come for a visit to the States. Following our visit, we learned that his ladyfriend left him after fifteen years for another person. The reason was the same as I had experienced: Horst was a very self-centered person who hardly appreciated any good intentions.

A few years later, his goal of visiting the U.S. one more time came through. We had assured him that he could come anytime and that we had enough space in our house to welcome and accommodate him. At that time we lived in Germantown, Wisconsin.

He came in the summer of 1999 with Sigrid, his new ladyfriend, who was a nurse. His health had worsened. I was in shock when we met him at the Chicago airport. The drive home, usually about two hours, took us three hours. Twice we had to stop because he could not sit anymore and needed to use facilities because of his poorly functioning bladder, the result of prostate surgery.

Upon arrival in Germantown, he preferred to relax at home and not move around too much. We had the chance to talk about our relationship. He admitted that he made mistakes in not treating me appropriately. He also could not understand why Karin had left him. My only answer was, "Please look in the mirror and ask yourself that very question."

In 2002 I learned that Horst had died a very lonely man. A neighbor lady had the keys to the house. She frequently checked on him. One day she found Horst lying dead on the kitchen floor.

Horst never had close friends. His daughter hardly visited him because of the estranged relationship following the divorce of her parents in 1977. Everything seemed to be a secret, especially money matters—he had a bank account in Switzerland. Besides him, only his sister had the account code. She never touched it, even after his death.

Horst had enough money, but he could not buy himself happiness, and I suppose, in one way, justice was done.

Ordinary Woman

Chapter 12
Brazilian and German Connection

Horst Cohn is the person I hold dearest and I would not miss to include him in my story.

I was offered a job in Hamburg at the publishing house Jahreszeiten Verlag—Gruner & Jahr. It was an interesting opportunity as I was a supervisor in one of the departments. I was responsible for the fashion and travel areas. Suddenly, the door was open for me, and I met the most interesting people while organizing a European Junior Fashion Show in Frankfurt. I was also able to use my knowledge of Polish and some Russian, as an interpreter, since models from Eastern European countries attended this show as well.

The publishing house had a travel agency. Because we needed exotic places for photo shoots, I was asked to go on a cruise to search for sunny places. At that time, only Italian vessels offered tours. Such vessels are no comparison to the present ships which accommodate more than five thousand passengers. The cruise I took accommodated about five hundred people. I had to take the train to Genoa, where I embarked the ship. I got a first-class cabin and got quickly acquainted with the crew. At a stop in Naples I was introduced to a local travel agent who took me by car to Sorrento, a small town in Campania in southern Italy. During the one-day stay, passengers had the choice either to take a ferry to the Island of Capri, or drive by car or train to Sorrento. I chose Sorrento because its beauty and surroundings. The town overlooks the bay and the water was clear and blue. Carlos, the agent, arranged two bungalows for our stay—one bedroom brick houses with small kitchens and big terraces overlooking the sea.

In the evening, we had dinner and some wine and could hear the noise in the dark from the boats that were approaching the port. The next day, we had meetings with the resort's owner and I got all the details our company needed. We had to rush back to Naples so I would not miss the vessel. I finished the cruise by stopping in Mallorca, Tunis, Sicily, and going back to Genoa. I took the train to Hamburg.

Back home, friends invited me to a birthday party where I was introduced to a gentleman who had just arrived from Brazil. He was of German descent, but had lived in Sao Paulo since 1933.

One of his parents was Jewish, and therefore, it became necessary for his family to leave Germany because of the danger under the Nazis. Many years later, after the war, he returned annually to Germany for few a months on business. That's why he attended his friend's birthday party. It was in February 1970, and I just returned from a trip and was a little exhausted, but did not want to disappoint my friends by staying away. I definitely would have missed the opportunity to meet a most interesting person.

His name was Mr. Cohn, and he arrived late because of traffic delays. The doorbell rang and the hostess rushed to welcome the new guest. When I saw him, I just thought:

"Wow! What a handsome man!"

He was maybe twenty years my senior, very attractive, tall, athletic and elegant. His complexion indicated that he originated from one of the southern countries. He was introduced to me formally.

"Please meet Mr. Horst Cohn, who recently arrived from Brazil on business," the host said.

"Pleasure to meet you as well, I am Irmgard Bothmer." (This is my real first name. Bothmer is my maiden name). We shook hands and started a conversation during which the guest told me that Cohn was a Jewish name. He explained to me that in 1933, due to Nazi development, the family had left Germany. He settled in Brazil, while his parents and brother immigrated to other countries. He knew that his parents had died later, but he never found his brother.

Horst Cohn was well educated and lectured at different Universities, but mainly he was a businessman. Many years had passed after World War II until he felt comfortable to travel back to Germany. His destination and connection was always Hamburg, the city with international flair. He also belonged to Freemasonry, as did my friend, Wilhelm, the host.

Because he anticipated staying in Hamburg for six months, he rented an apartment in a nice neighborhood that was close to the place I worked at that time. We started to see each other after work. Each time I came, there was a cup of coffee and a drink waiting. The apartment was small but cozy. He talked about his life. He was married to a Brazilian lady whom he admired, but who had had health problems since she was a young girl.

She was deprived of having a child; therefore, they adopted a baby boy. The child brought happiness and pride to their lives, and he was a very good student.

Horst and I enjoyed each other's company when we went for dinner or dancing. To dance with him was heaven. When the orchestra played a waltz by Johann Strauss and we started to dance, everybody's eyes followed us. They probably were asking themselves:

"Who are they? Father and daughter? Or?"

Horst initiated my interest into German literature. His favorite writer was Wolfgang Goethe, and often I listened when he read a book aloud. We went together to the theater and opera, which I enjoyed very much. He got me interested in culture.

I had not been to southern Germany. Therefore, when Horst asked me to join him on such a trip, I was just excited. We drove in his car, first to the mountains, the Alps, and stopped in Mittenwald, a town not far from Garmisch Pattenkirchen. Those towns are known as Olympic ski resorts. Horst made a reservation for two rooms in one of the Pensions (a Bed and Breakfast). He treated me like his daughter and never made any advances towards me. He walked with me and explained to me all the beautiful and richly decorated churches and introduced me to the southern kitchen. I could not get enough of the unbelievable landscape.

While we continued, he showed me another historical site, the Heidelberg Castle. Everybody who visited Germany had to go to Heidelberg, which is a university town with pubs and cafes where students meet in the evenings. The castle ruin is on a hill. The view from above took my breath away. The castle gardens were originally designed by a French engineer who integrated waterfalls, terraces, statues and beautiful flowers. The tour through the old town was wonderful. We drove north along the river Rhein, surrounded by vineries and castle ruins on hills. It was a very romantic journey that I still enjoy today if there is enough time during our annual visits to Germany.

The time came when Horst had to return to Brazil. I really enjoyed being with him. I could count on him whenever there was a need. He also felt he had to protect and guide me. We promised to stay in touch by exchanging tapes and letters.

"I will be back next year," he promised at the airport in Hamburg. Suddenly, I felt empty. To overcome this feeling, I threw myself into my work, which meant traveling as well.

We saw each other one more time a year later, but only briefly, due to my work re-location and assignments. He dedicated some poems and stories to me, which I still cherish. The correspondence paused, and finally letters were returned with the remark, "Recipient deceased." I never learned what happened.

This chapter is dedicated to Horst just to say, "Thank you for the wonderful time, for opening the world to me and for being the best friend I ever had."

Chapter 13
Return to the Roots in 1969

I never lost touch with my birthplace, and specifically, the city Wroclaw where I spent my school years.

Over the years, my elementary school teacher, Pani Janina, who passed away in April 2011, as well as her daughter and granddaughters, grew very close to my heart. From the moment we left Poland in December 1955, and the city Wroclaw (formally Breslau), we kept a correspondence going without interruption. One reason was to not lose the knowledge of the Polish language, and the other was to keep her informed about my new environment, such as country, people and family.

My command of Polish—reading and writing—was still perfect after ten years (1965), but my speaking skills had eroded. When my school friend Rita called me from Vienna in 1965 to tell me that she had just immigrated, I had a problem answering in Polish. and started to stutter. With her help, such as visiting each other and continuous phone calls, I quickly got back on track.

I visited Poland for the very first time to celebrate New Year's Eve in 1969. I arranged it with the tourist agency, and joined a tour to Warsaw with a group of twenty other people. I was a little nervous since I learned that tourists were observed by the secret service and were not able to move about freely at that time. Well, I took the chance and the trip was a success.

Prior to New Year's Eve, I confided in few people about my plan to take the train and go to Wroclaw. My teacher knew of my intention and she promised to pick me up at the train station. It was a night train.

Fourteen years had passed by, and my concern was whether I would recognize my teacher. The unbelievable happened. The train approached the station and slowly came to a stop. I opened the compartment window to look for her. Across the open window on the platform a gentleman was standing. At this moment the question popped out of my mouth:

"Are you Mr. Lupaczyk?" (husband of my teacher). With a big smile he answered:

"Yes, that's me."

Never in my life had I seen this man before. It was unbelievable. His wife was there as well, but she waited at the main entrance. The greeting was tearful and filled with joy.

We took a taxi. Because I was so excited being home again, I kindly asked the driver, "May I try to give you driving directions just to see if I still remember?"

"Certainly. Go ahead," he answered with a big smile.

I found the way to the destination and was proud of myself. It was after midnight when we arrived. Since I had only a day to spend with them before returning to Warsaw, they put me to bed right away for a few hours. After breakfast, we took a tour through the city, and in the afternoon I already was back on the train to Warsaw. It was a short, but sincere, visit. At that time, I did not know that two years later I would be back on an assignment in Warsaw.

In February 1972, I started my work in Warsaw as a representative for the German Trade Mission, and later the German Embassy.

During this time I visited Wroclaw many times. I got to see other places and cities as well. This assignment will be covered in details in another chapter. It will also cover my transfer to Chicago, where I was employed with the Consulate General of the Federal Republic of Germany.

The next private trip to Poland was in 1988. Germany was still divided, and I knew that the checkpoints on the east side were not pleasant. I took a train from Hannover to Warsaw. The duration was not the eight hours as the schedule indicated, but thirteen long hours.

Our train wagon was disconnected from the train and moved to a deadlock rail. For over four hours we waited to be moved again. Passport, customs control and currency exchange people visited each compartment. Finally we were reconnected and moved forward. Another control check occurred at the Polish border, but it was much more pleasant.

In Warsaw, two families were expecting me at the main station and everyone was eager to be the first to host me. Finally, I made the decision, and everybody was happy. A girlfriend, Teresa, came from Kielce to see me because of my limited time. I could not go to her. It was very emotional. I met Teresa during my hospitalization with knee surgery in 1973. She had suffered a bad bus accident and had to undergo seven surgeries. We kept in close contact, and still do.

During this five-day Warsaw visit I had the chance again to go to Wroclaw with one of my girlfriends. We took a morning train from Warsaw and returned the next day. I never missed a visit with my teacher.

In 1995, I scheduled another trip to Poland. Because my husband Rudi and I were on assignment in Germany, I decided to show Rudi the country I was born in and went to school. Rudi had never been to Poland. We took a car and drove to Wroclaw.

It was still a long and exhausting trip with waiting times at the border. Finally, we arrived. Rudi was very impressed. The architecture and history was overwhelming. At that time the whole city was under construction. Finally funds were released to restore streets, the city hall, and downtown in preparation for the Holy Year, which was celebrated a year later. We enjoyed the restaurants, shopping and sightseeing. Marta, the daughter of my teacher, took time and showed us around.

Polish women are known as being beautiful and fashion oriented. My interest was directed in visiting boutiques and designer ateliers. Naturally, shoes made in Italy caught my eyes. Rudi, being a camera collector, was drawn to antique stores and was lucky to find special lenses for one of his cameras.

We added one more trip to our travel experience and were accompanied by my mother and sister. It was my mother's last journey and turned out to be very sad. We realized that dementia had kicked in, and her memory was gone. My sister, however, who had not been to Poland since we left in December 1955, enjoyed the trip tremendously.

Chapter 14
The Moscow Love Story

Travel to Russia is a unique opportunity to get acquainted with Russian history and culture. Russia spans eleven time zones and two continents and is one of the most beautiful countries in the world. This is a great country with an array of rivers, forests and towering mountains.

My first visit to Russia as a private citizen came in 1969 to celebrate the Christmas and New Year's season together with a tourist group. The group I joined was outstanding. People were nice and easygoing. We enjoyed each other's company. The program included sightseeing, museums, theater and sleigh rides. It was bitter cold, and we all were glad to have our fur or winter coats on hand. I made friends and loved to be among this group. We also were introduced to the Russian kitchen by stopping at several ethnic restaurants.

Considering that the country was ruled by Communists, we were pleasantly surprised to receive such excellent service. We all realized that none of the Russian people could afford expensive restaurant visits unless they had Communist Party privileges. Also, they were not allowed to enter a hotel or bar which was just for foreigners

Traveling to Moscow we had to start from the East Berlin's Schoeneberg Airport. The Russian Ilysin airplane was old, very noisy and uncomfortable.

We landed in Moscow's Sheremetyevo International Airport. There was strict passport control, and a charted bus that was shaky and unheated brought us to the Hotel Rossija. At that time, it was one of the largest hotels with a prestigious location. It accommodated about 5,500 guests. From the hotel a short walk led to Red Square and the Kremlin with its Congress Hall and Bolshoi Theater.

Upon arrival, everyone had to leave their passports at the reception desk. They were returned on the day of departure. We were informed, "This is the general procedure to be registered." Everybody knew that the secret service was checking everyone out.

I fell in love with this city. We walked at night to the Red Square, which was fully illuminated, and the favored meeting spot for love birds. It was very romantic. During the daytime, the square was filled with people who lined up to enter the Lenin Mausoleum. Lenin was an idol, who with the Bolsheviks, had overthrown the Tsarist regime.

Performances at the Bolshoi Theater or in the Congress Hall at the Kremlin were very impressive. This Hall sat 5,000 people per performance. Everything seemed to be big and wide. Police patrols were everywhere. Since Russians are known to drink a lot, police made sure that no drunks were visible on the street or bothering visitors. We had no problems going for a walk at night in parks as well, as parks were also securely illuminated.

We had bilingual Russian tourist guides who were outstanding. They answered our questions as far as they were allowed. They led us to stores which were for foreigners only, where we could buy caviar and Krymskoye champagne. We bought fur hats, which helped us in the bitterly cold climate. The New Year's Eve celebration was a blast. We celebrated Father Frost, a tradition in Russia instead of Christmas, as well.

Ordinary Woman

Two days later we returned to Germany with wonderful memories and a new experience from behind the Iron Curtain. The German tourist agency offered me a position as tourist guide, which I gladly accepted. I just had the desire to return to Russia.

While being on assignment in Moscow I met many interesting people. Most of them came on business and spent their "waiting time" in hotels. "Waiting time" meant being on call for meetings with Russian government officials to discuss contracts or other deals. Sometimes, from the time offers were submitted until the actual meeting took place, the waiting took up to three weeks.

The first person I met and got acquainted was David Short, a dark-haired, chubby man who was very English and who represented the Hewlett Packard company. He was very friendly, but also strange in behavior and conversation. I had a hard time judging or reading him. There were moments when he looked right through me. I would call him a "cold fish."

I still wasn't fluent in English, so I asked him, "David, could you please correct me, so I say it properly?" He answered, "I am not doing it; it is against the etiquette. One does not correct another person's language." This man had no manners.

Later, David introduced me to a young fellow from Oxford while we spent an evening in the hotel bar. His name was Richard Thompson. He was about thirty years old, very flamboyant, and knew how to dress and present himself. He represented a company named Perkin-Elmer, and was dealing with the Russian government as well.

He asked me for a dance, as a balalaika trio was playing a beautiful waltz. We both seemed to be very compatible. A dinner followed, as did frequent theater visits to the Bolshoi Theater, where he introduced me to Earl Tolia Uvariov, one of the first-row violinists in the orchestra. Invitations to the artists homes followed. One was from the tenor Denis Karialov, who invited us to a dinner party. Such parties were filled with warmth, sentiment and music.

Richard was born in middle-class Oxford in 1941. His father, a football-mad chemist, was working on secret spectroscopy studies, analyzing German airplane fuels for the Ministry of Supply. He later was knighted, and became Foreign Secretary of Royal Society (Britain's senior Scientific Ambassador). Richard's father was determined and conservative, and prone to brief, irrational rages.

By contrast, his mother was a liberal classics teacher, softer, with a giggly sense of humor and a genuine laugh, and much more approachable and fun to be with. I never met either one, but that's how Richard described his parents.

As to Richard's education, he finished four years of study in chemistry. Science, music and languages were his hobbies. He learned the Russian language, which made his life easier while in Russia on assignment, and which became a major tool in his espionage activities.

At the time we met I did not know anything about those activities. His artistic and musical abilities opened doors in his spying life. Richard played jazz clarinet, which helped him make contacts.

During the days I took care of arriving and departing tourists, but in the evenings I kept company with Richard. Rumors spread quickly that we were lovers and inseparable. By all means this was true. Jealous people reported it to the KGB, but being lovers was not a crime. We behaved properly, did not discuss any politics, and minded our own business.

While we both had a break from work, Richard and I decided to take a trip. We had one thought in mind, "Let's go to Sotchi," a Black Sea resort. The town of Sotchi is situated at the foot of the Caucasus Mountain range on the Black Sea. The trip had to be booked through the Russian travel agency Intourist. Little did I know that additional arrangements had been made for us. It started at the airport. We were treated as first-class passengers so we could embark the aircraft first and sit right behind the pilot. There were no dividers between first-and economy-class. The seats were very hard and narrow, and only juice was served. The same thing happened upon arrival. Richard and I disembarked first. Everyone else had to wait.

Suddenly, a gentleman approached us. He wanted to confirm our names and stated that he was assigned to drive us to the hotel. First he stopped at the Hotel Leningrad where I was booked, and then Hotel Magnolia, a class lower where Richard was supposed to stay. It was a surprise that they booked us in two different hotels. Of course, we wanted to be at the same hotel, but the Hotel Leningrad was not willing to accommodate us both. Richard decided then, "Let's check with the Magnolia for such possibility." We were lucky, and my luggage was moved to the Hotel Magnolia.

The warm weather and the southern atmosphere added to a comfortable and relaxing time. We swam, learned about the area and dined out. Each time we stepped out of the hotel, a black Wolga car and a driver seemed to be waiting for us. It was unusual, but we got used to it. Certainly, we took advantage of it and knew that the driver was a KGB agent. But this did not bother us "tourists," and we made the best of it.

After a week we returned to Moscow and continued with our tasks. The first to leave Moscow and to return to his home office was Richard. In June 1971, I was transferred to Famagusta (on the Greek Island Cypress) to substitute for a vacationing co-worker. I missed Richard terribly because we had gotten so close to each other. We exchanged letters.

In August 1971, I was back in Russia, but this time in Leningrad. Here we met again, then later in Germany, and one more time in Poland in 1973.

This relationship was indeed a love affair which I imagined would develop into a serious commitment. This was to be only a dream, as we both were torn apart by our jobs in different countries.

In February 1972, my new assignment was in the West German Embassy in Warsaw, and in February 1974, I was transferred to Chicago. Richard was in Brussels where he had just started a job with an American chemical company. The contact faded under those circumstances. A few calls were still exchanged, and then there was silence—until thirty years later.

A business contact from England seemed to know where to find Prof. Richard Thompson. I telephoned him and when he answered, "Here is Professor Richard from Oxford," I knew that I had found the pretty, flamboyant young man from the Russian time. That was in 2003, and Richard was sixty-two years old. We started to exchange messages and catch up on the missed thirty years via email and phone calls. He submitted to me his biography and asked me to read the chapters he had tried to publish. He hoped it would be a script for a soap opera. Indeed, the content was very juicy. To some of those chapters he added photos in order to backup stories of his sexual exploits. His efforts to publish the stories were met with rejections.

I did cut off our communication because I was too conservative for him. His emails were nasty and contradicting. The last message I got about him came in 2004 from a neighbor lady who had access to his email. She said he was a dying man who was surrounded by "a sexy nurse and lady doctor." This was proof that besides his handicaps (blindness, spine problems and stomach cancer), his sexual desire was still intact. Whether he indeed died, I don't know.

This bittersweet chapter is closed for me.

Chapter 15
Two Months in Leningrad
(St. Petersburg)

Following the two months on the Island Cypress in 1971, I returned to Russia, but this time not to Moscow, but to Leningrad, (St. Petersburg). After the warm temperatures on Cypress, I had to get used to the colder environment and breezy air.

During my assignment in Moscow 1971, my first visit to Leningrad was coordinated by the tourist office, and was set for one week. Within that week I had already been introduced to the beauty of this city. The name St Petersburg originates from the time it was founded in 1703. Following the Russian Revolution and Bolshevism, it was renamed Leningrad. This city, with its outlet to the sea, was and is very important for Russia's future development from both a strategic and economic point of view. I had the chance to visit and learn more about Leningrad during a later assignment as a tourist guide.

St. Petersburg is a city built on water, with a complex network of canals and waterways that are spanned by countless bridges. The River Neva is its main artery. To walk along the Neva is to experience one of Europe's most palatial sections of the river. From the grand homes of the Tsar to historic squares, the embankment is St. Petersburg at its finest.

A row of splendid mansions that overlooked the river were not open to the public at that time. The palaces, still untouched by modern restoration, offered a real insight into how St. Petersburg must have looked in the nineteenth century at the height of its imperial glory.

The tourists enjoyed trips to the Summer Garden, which is perhaps St Petersburg's loveliest and oldest park. We were told by the Russian guide that the park was laid out for Peter the Great with fountains, pavilions and a geometrical plan to resemble the park at Versailles. It became a stomping ground for nineteenth century ladies and gentlemen of leisure. People are proud to have such elegant places to show to visitors from all over Europe and other countries.

I was fortunate to visit the modest, two-story Summer Palace in the northeastern corner of the park. It was St Petersburg's first palace and was built for Peter between 1704 and 1714.

The history of the place describes its inner look. The walls depict Russian naval victories, and many rooms contain early eighteenth century furnishings. Architects and artisans were brought from all over Europe to build it. By Czar Peter's death in 1725, his city had a huge population, and ninety percent of Russia's foreign trade passed through it. Its access to the Baltic Sea, and connections to other "Hansa" cities helped it develop into a trading center.

The Neva River is the romantic meeting point at night not only for "love birds," but also for everyone who appreciates romantic moments. All bridges are raised for ship traffic at two in the morning. The bridges are illuminated, as are historic buildings along the river.

I remember having a tourist group placed in the Hotel Leningrad located on the other side of the river. As a tourist guide I had to visit them, socialize and discuss the next day's schedules. Often it got late and I had to rush out before bridges were lifted in order to get back to my Hotel Europe. I had to walk through the park, which was romantic because of the beautiful, indirect illumination of its bushes, but at night hardly anybody walked there. I felt secure knowing that the Russian police were strict regarding drunks and bums strolling or sleeping on the streets and in the parks.

One night, however, returning late, I suddenly heard steps. Somebody was walking behind me and kept coming closer. It startled me a bit but I kept walking. A few moments later a gentleman was next to me and asked in Russian whether he could accompany me to wherever I was going, just to be on the safe side. He was a very nice person. I thanked him and we continued while he told me about himself and the city that was his home. In no time we arrived at my hotel. He said goodbye while kissing my hand as a respectful sign of admiration, and then he left. I never saw him again. The Russian people, no matter how rich or poor, are raised to show respect and admiration, specifically in the social life. Honestly, I loved it!

I missed the phenomenon known as the White Nights, which appears in the month of June. It is not unique to St Petersburg. Finland, the neighboring country, is a great experience as well. People say there could be nothing more romantic than to walk along the banks of the city's rivers and canals. At that time, night is almost broad daylight

The time in St. Petersburg was too short to experience and visit all places. The most famous Hermitage Museum was closed due to some restorations. With my tourist groups I was able to visit Tsarskoe Selo (Tsars Village), located twenty-five kilometers south of St. Petersburg, as well as Catherine Palace and Alexander Palace. All those are set among beautiful parklands.

Not everything was open to the public, but what we could see was incredibly beautiful. Many things were destroyed during the revolution, such as the Great Staircase, installed in 1860, and the Great Hall, a masterpiece of Baroque architecture. Still, you could imagine the feeling walking down the

Great Stairs. Today, thirty years later, definitely all the restorations have been completed, and it is my wish to again visit this outstanding city.

St. Petersburg, as well as Moscow, is proud of its cultural achievements. Many theaters, opera and museums can be visited. Whenever there was an opportunity, I attended concerts or ballet performances. The atmosphere in the concert hall or opera house was elegant and very pleasant. During the intermission, champagne, wine and snacks were offered. There was also a chance to meet the performers. I loved it because that was how the Russian people celebrated and enjoyed those moments. People felt free to talk and embrace, as they were not being observed by authorities.

The two months went by too fast, but another assignment in Germany was waiting. It was a very exciting and educational time. I met interesting people and learned about the history and tradition of this city, which I cherish. Today, after forty years, I suggested to Rudi that we visit this wonderful city and re-live the past experiences.

Chapter 16
Assignment in Poland

Upon acceptance at the Office for Foreign Affairs in Bonn, Germany, I was told that my assignment would be in Warsaw. I still had to pass an exam in the Polish language, which I did. My household and personal belongings were loaded to a mover's truck and sealed, ready to hit the road. I finalized a car purchase at a dealership who supplied members of the Office for Foreign Affairs with special terms. I had chosen a sport model from Ford Europe called Capri. At the time, this car was very much in style and I loved it.

After four weeks at the main office in Bonn, it was time to move on, and yes, I admit, I was a little nervous. Seventeen years had passed since my family had left Poland under difficult circumstances, and I was going back. There was one handicap to overcome. East Germany, with its Communist regime, did not allow us to pass through the country unless we had specific permits. In this case, I had chosen to drive to Munich, stay overnight with my girlfriend, and continue the next day driving through the Czech Republic towards Poland. It took me about fourteen hours. I arrived in Wroclaw, and that night I stayed in one of the newer hotels. I had no problems at the borders, everybody was very helpful. Warsaw was another five hours drive. I had never been to Warsaw before, but the directions given to me were perfect and I did not get lost. My starting date for work was February 1, 1972.

In Poland, West Germany was represented by a Trade Mission which had to be transferred into an embassy after three months. The governments of both countries had been talking to each other for quite some time and had negotiated several terms of cooperation, such as embassy employee issues, visiting official sites and economic cooperation.

Finally, the first ambassador and his staff arrived. Official documents with full power of their governments were presented in Warsaw, as well as in Bonn.

At first we were a small group, but we expanded tremendously later on. Transferred from Germany were the ambassador, deputy counsel, consular officers and bilingual secretaries. Local employees were secretaries, clerical personnel, janitors, and drivers.

For our safety, we had personnel from the German Federal Border Enforcement (comparable here with Marine units). Their tasks were to protect the Embassy and its personnel inside the compound. Polish soldiers were posted outside for security.

Two buildings had been leased and restored. The location was in one of the best areas of Warsaw, a subdivision called Saska Kepa, and known as the Diplomat's Subdivision. The Polish government made sure that the area was safeguarded. Around-the-clock guards were on duty. Those guards were there to provide us protection, but also to observe and spy on us foreigners. I was lucky to find an apartment in the same area just ten minutes away from the office.

There were a lot of robberies and burglaries in the area, so I had to take special precautions, such as putting double locks on my doors and iron bars in front of the windows. The apartment was on the main floor, and was an easy target. Cars had to be parked in the garage overnight, otherwise parts would have been missing the next day—windshield wipers, tire caps and such. This was the time when stores were empty

Ordinary Woman

and one could get spare parts for cars only through connections.

I got very friendly with the guard on my street. Quite often I returned home late at night from a banquet or party. My garage was one block away, and sometimes I left the car parked on the street, and the guards kept an eye on it. They also accompanied me to my apartment door, and prior to my entering, they checked the surroundings for intruders. I was not shy about giving them a Thank You gift—cartons of cigarettes—even though I knew they were spying on me as well.

I learned to be as open as I could with the people of the Secret Service, who in the long run, protected me and saved my life.

In the embassy we were covered with work for twelve hours a day. First we had to establish contacts with the Secretary of State, Department of Cultural Affairs, as well as the Department of Economic Affairs. Many ministerial meetings took place, and there were also visit exchanges between embassies.

The time went by so fast, and unfortunately, we did not realize that we had an enemy among our employees. It was a lady who had been transferred from Germany. She was trained to code and decode confidential messages from headquarters.

At that time, I worked for the deputy counsel, Dr. Sikora, a very intelligent and bright gentleman who spoke five languages fluently. He was not easy to work with and I never liked his eye impression. His eyes were penetrating. He often stared into space, which scared me.

The Lady X managed to get involved with him, not because she fell in love with him, but because she wanted my job. At the end, she succeeded because Dr. Sikora seemed to be blind to the reality of who and what she was. They were sexually involved, which destroyed his marriage. I felt so sorry for his wife, who was the most gentle, lovely and sincere lady, and who dedicated her life to her family and her children's education.

Months later when Dr. Sikora and Lady X disappeared, (they had been secretly deported), we were told that she was a spy for East Germany. A trial took place, Dr. Sikora was suspended, and he never returned as an employee.

When I lost my job working for Dr. Sikora, I was transferred to the second building, which served as consulate general, and I learned they needed me there more because I spoke Polish fluently. Another secretary, Barbara, and I were the only employees transferred from Germany who were fluent in Polish.

The consulate was unbelievably busy. People from all over the country would gather in the early morning and patiently wait until our doors opened.

There were two specific reasons for them to come: first, to apply for family reunion with their relatives in West Germany, and second, to register for restitution payments for losses suffered at the hands of the Nazis and for payments for having been herded into Nazi concentration camps.

In the first case, people had to prove that they indeed were of German descent. They had to supply documents, which were sent to Germany for investigation. This was a time-consuming process that could drag on for months.

The restitution cases were sad and very emotional. Polish and Jewish people shared their stories, which Barbara and I had to interpret. Again, proof and witnesses had to be submitted. Those people visited us two and three times. We had no idea how much those people must have suffered. Sometimes those clients got nasty and impatient because we could not furnish them with the correct and helpful answers. I remember one specific case. A gentleman came to us to apply for restitution. As we learned through the investigations, he already received a particular amount paid by the Geneva Convention, and, therefore, was not entitled to another payment.

He was angry, if not furious, and threatened me, as the interpreter. Shortly after he left our office, a security person informed me that this particular person had crashed into my car, which had been parked in front of our building. The Polish security guards witnessed it, and an immediate arrest took place. This man was never again allowed to enter our building.

Barbara had a mental breakdown. She could not handle this depressing work, so we had to release her for a few weeks. She had to take sick leave and, consequently, my workday grew to fourteen hours or more.

Once in a while we had visitors with the craziest demands. A Russian fellow appeared one day and requested to speak to our ambassador, who at the time was out of town on a special assignment. Then this man asked to meet with the next person in line. He met with my supervisor, the Deputy Consul General. The reason for this visit was "to mobilize the German Army to carry out a raid on the Soviet Union." He presented a detailed map of the Soviet Union marked with German flags, which indicated where the raids could take place.

We could not believe our eyes and ears. This man must have been out of his mind. We were polite, listened and acknowledged his demonstration. Then he identified himself with both Russian and Polish passports.

After a while he left with the words, "I will come back expecting an answer given by the ambassador."

We discussed this internally and decided that he was mentally disturbed, and we hoped to never see him again. But we were totally wrong. It did not take too long for him to come back. Neither our ambassador nor my supervisor were available. The man was angry and had a fit of rage. I tried very politely to calm him down and explained that we had informed our authorities about his suggestions and plans, but that we did not get any response. He did not want to listen, and grabbed my arm with the words, "I will kill you." My co-workers stood around speechless and did not know what to do, as certainly this was an unusual case. I continued to talk to him like a child, and finally he released my arm and left. I was shaking for the very first time because it was a serious threat. Without informing our authorities, I called the Polish Ministry of Interior (Secret Service) and reported this man. They caught up with him and he never bothered us again.

I learned later that from that moment on, the Polish Secret Service had arranged special protection for me.

Some of the Polish civilians tried to interfere with our lives. In order to get money from us, they caused traffic accidents, in particular when one of my colleagues was behind the wheel. Somehow a police car arrived quickly. After I spoke to them in Polish and explained the situation, the case was clarified immediately and we were on our way.

It happened also when I was driving with the Deputy Consul Dr. Ellerkmann and his family to visit the famous bison park called Białowieża National Park. It is the largest natural forest remaining in Europe. Many parts of the park have preserved their natural character. There are thousand species, but most famously, the European bison.

The trip was supposed to take us about five hours. We had a reservation at the hotel in the park and had another hour still to drive. We drove with Dr. Ellerkmann's car, an Audi. The road through the villages was empty because it was a weekend and farmers were not in the fields. I was sitting in the passenger seat with my bandaged knee following a previous surgery. Mrs. Ellerkmann and their son were sitting in the backseats. Suddenly a motorcyclist approached from the opposite lane and made a turn in front of us without any turning sign. It was just a moment of seconds when we saw him and tried to brake. It was too late. His motorcycle smashed into our car, the bike got stuck between the two front wheels and the rider was catapulted above our car and into a ditch. We were shocked, my boss was pale and I thought he would faint. Due to this crash I did hurt my injured knee. The little boy was thrown from the back to the front between the seats and hit his head on the dashboard.

Immediately we got out of the car and searched for the motorcyclist. He was dead. As I mentioned, the road was empty before, but suddenly, dozens of people appeared. They were yelling, "These foreigners think that the road belongs to them!" They cursed and threatened us as well. Thankfully the police came. They investigated the accident, measured our braking tracks and recorded what we had witnessed. It was definitely not our fault. The motorcyclist, a farmer, did not carry a helmet and did not show a turning sign. The police ordered the spectators to lend a hand, lift the car, and remove the motorcycle from underneath. Then they arranged that the car was towed to a nearby repair shop to make it drivable. Dr. Ellerkmann had never before experienced an accident. He was in shock and wanted to return to Warsaw. The policeman urged him not to do it, but to continue to the hotel, relax and make plans for the next day. We followed the instruction, but instead of visiting the park next day we returned home. We appreciated the help and friendliness of the police.

Whenever I traveled in Poland I was shadowed by a Secret Service agent. I felt okay because I did not have anything to hide. Sometimes, my shadows and I would accidentally meet in a restaurant, and I told them face-to-face that I was aware that they were following me. They usually smiled and offered me a cup of coffee, but they never said anything.

Poland offers so many interesting historical and remarkable architectural objects and places. It was unbelievable what I was able to learn while traveling around. There were wonderful castles that had been restored and opened as public museums.

Due to the work I was assigned to, it was important for me to visit one of the concentration camps, Majdanek, which was open to visitors. But in this case, I needed protection and could not take my foreign car. I was told that because Germans were still hated, I would be in danger. Further, I was warned that visiting survivors of the camp might attack me. Two Polish friends accompanied and showed me around. It was the most horrible place I have ever seen. Barracks still in place served as showcases displaying clothes, jewelry, golden teeth and hair taken from the prisoners before they were forced either to the gas chamber or otherwise executed. I saw the gas chamber and I saw the fireplaces where bodies were cremated. After the war, the dumped ashes were later preserved, and a monument was dedicated to the victims of the Nazi regime. I got sick and needed fresh air. On the way back, we stopped at another former camp where high-ranking Polish officers were tortured and killed, and I will never forget what I saw and how sick I got to my stomach.

Although I was busy with work, I would host dinner parties for guests from different countries, as well as for my Polish friends. There were restrictions in communicating with Polish people, and the Secret Service observed the activities of my guests. Unfortunately, some of my guests tried to make illegal deals with foreigners who traded art and other costly items. Eventually, the attorney who was hired by the consulate to solve legal cases was suddenly arrested for such illegal trading.

Upon his arrest, we searched for him because we didn't know what had occurred. We learned later from his wife that he had caused the danger himself. He went to prison, but it was too much for him, and he later committed suicide.

From then on, I limited my invitations and kept in touch with just certain friends whom I trusted and with whom I felt comfortable. Unfortunately, the brother of my best girlfriend, who was courting me, turned out to be an agent who spied on me and delivered information about my high-profile guests to Polish authorities. It was a shocking surprise when I learned of it several years later.

Because of the previously described embassy spy affair, German authorities wanted my co-worker Barbara and I to move out of Poland in order to avoid any further contact with the Polish Secret Service. Word of the spy affair had already spread around, but we had no real details. Barbara ended up in Brussels, Belgium, and I was assigned to the Consulate General in Chicago.

The reason for this overnight transfer was based on the political relationship between East Germany, Poland and Russia. Russia manipulated countries behind the Iron Curtain, and East Germany and Poland hated each other.

I left Poland in early December 1973 on short notice. I was not even allowed to pack my household items. That was done later for me by consulate employees. It was not easy to leave my friends behind. At that time, I realized that I had reconnected with my childhood memories and that I loved Poland. I promised myself to return and to keep in touch with friends, which I have done to this day.

I kept my promise and have gone back to Poland several times. In May, 2011, I returned to Poland and reconnected with longtime friends. Not only did I visit the places I knew, but also places that I previously had not had the chance to see. It was a wonderful journey. It was fun to visit with friends, but I was sad when I again left my home.

Chapter 17
Assignment in Poland Part Two
The Spy Affair

The real reason for my leaving Poland was based on a spy affair which was disclosed years later in magazines such as Der Spiegel, Quick and other famous newspapers. Here is what I found out in that regard upon my return to Germany:

My previous co-worker, Gerda Schroeter, as were many others, was hired as an agent by the East German State Security Police, called the SSD. Herbert Schroeter, her lover, and later husband, got her there in 1966. Herbert was an experienced officer whose duty was to train newcomers in foreign policy. Trips to Washington and London seemed to be very promising, especially "out of love."

Since she never was able to travel to the western countries, it was exciting for her and her companion to stay in the best hotels. She attended cultural events, and had spending money. In other words she was a decoy-bird. Following an intensive training she found a job at the State Department of the Federal Republic of Germany in Bonn. She was placed in the Department of Telecommunications. A security check did not give any indication to the authorities that she was a spy. Her ability to read ciphered information had opened the door for her spying activities. The Cold War was raging at the time, and Eastern European countries were hostile towards West Germany. Gerda continued to work in the TELCO Department and was described as loyal. Nobody at that time knew that she was traveling three times a week from Cologne to East Berlin using an express train to deliver highly secure information.

One of her first big assignments was to deliver NATO security documents to the East Germans. For that she later was awarded a gold medal by the East Germans, who described it as her best achievement. Her words were:

"Here I was standing with the gold medal not even reading the in script on it. I was speechless. Later I learned that only 'acknowledged, recognized members of the State Security Police earn it.'" The medal was later taken away by Herbert with the words, "As soon as you live here with us, you will be able to carry it."

Gerda was transferred to Warsaw, where I was working, to replace an employee. She arrived in 1972, and was again placed in the telecommunication department. At that time, as I previously mentioned, I was working for the Deputy Ambassador, Dr. Sikora, who was not the easiest person to work for. He was very demanding, unjustified and secretive. His wife and children hardly stayed with him. He also separated himself from the Embassy staff in a way that rumors and suspicions circulated. Rumors abounded that he was sexually involved with Gerda, but there was still no word that Gerda took advantage of being with Dr. Sikora, who trusted her, and therefore she had access to many secret documents.

And then came this particular day when he announced that I should not work for him but be replaced by Gerda. I was speechless and in shock. Our honorary consul jumped in to rescue me and arranged for me to be an interpreter at the Polish-German consular building next door.

Months went by when, in late 1973, we realized that an affair had flourished between Gerda and Dr. Sikora. Suddenly, they both disappeared overnight. No questions were answered, but a few days later my co-worker Barbara and I were pressed to leave the country immediately. We learned in Germany how this affair had unfolded and that Gerda consequently surrendered to authorities. Dr.Sikora was suspended.

Chapter 18
Assignment in Poland Part Three
My Dear Friend Bozena

"How do I feel about writing?" It scares me to be honest in describing the meeting with my girlfriend before leaving Poland after a two-week vacation in May 2011. There were with so many vivid and refreshed memories. The time was short and compressed, but I had the need to see her no matter what.

I've known Bozena since 1973. I was introduced to her by her brother Piotr, whom I met at a party thrown by a common friend. Bozena and I liked each other from the moment we met. She told me, "I was born in 1947, got married and gave birth to my daughter, Ania, who was born in 1970." She continued: "My marriage was based on dishonesty and inconsolable matters, and we parted a year ago."

I listened to her, since I had the feeling that she needed someone to talk to. I told her: "That's quite a story you are telling me," and I asked her further, "What are you doing now in order to support you and your daughter?" She told me that she was working as a nurse and that her parents were watching little Ania.

I learned that she was living with her parents, which made it easier for her to care for the child. Her parents, whom I met along with her sister Kate, were very lovely and caring people who always welcomed me into their home. They lived in an apartment building that had been built before WW II, and which, fortunately, had not been destroyed, as had so many others. The house was in good shape and clean, and the main entrance was always locked, which kept intruders away.

On the weekends when I was not on call for the West German Embassy, Bozena showed me around Warsaw and the surrounding area. In the summertime, we spent weekends together either travelling, or swimming in a man-made lake. Because she was struggling, I tried my best to support her and make sure that little Ania had enough to wear. The stores were not furnished with decent merchandise, therefore, I brought items from Germany whenever I went back there to visit family or friends. I adored Ania and treated her as if she were mine.

Ania is now forty-one. When we saw her at her wedding in 2006, she mentioned in front of all her guests how lucky she was to call me Aunt Irma, and that she never forgot what I had done for her.

I left Warsaw in 1974 for an assignment in Chicago, but throughout the years I kept in touch with Bozena and mailed her packages with clothing for her and her daughter.

Bozena remarried in 1983. Her husband's name is Bartek, and he is ten years older than her. In 1987, their daughter Monica was born. I visited them in 1989 for few days while vacationing in Germany. At that time they had moved into an ugly, stinky, dirty high-rise building with a squeaky elevator. Their two-bedroom apartment was on the twelfth floor. It was an emotional and sincere visit. I liked Bozena's husband, a big and heavy person, very much. I called him Teddy Bear. We talked through the night and exchanged memories from the past.

From the moment I saw little Monica I realized that something was very wrong. Her face showed strange impressions, she made sounds which were not normal, and she seemed to have a bad temper. When I asked Bozena, "Is anything wrong with Monica?" she started to cry and said, "We still do not know exactly what is wrong and doctors are running tests."

Bozena was very depressed, and most of the time Bartek cared for the child. Later on I learned that Monica had Down Syndrome. It was a very sad situation and Bozena started to smoke and drink heavily.

I visited them again in 2006, when Rudi and I were invited to Ania's wedding. Bartek had purchased a house on the outskirts of Warsaw in order to be close to a special school where Monica was enrolled. The house was a two-story building with a big garden in the backyard. Inside it was nicely remodeled and furnished. We stayed there for few days before going to Ciechocinek for Ania's wedding. At that time, I saw Monica and I was shocked. She was nine years old, her figure had ballooned into an adult size of 20W, and I could hardly communicate with her. She also showed mood swings, which were disturbing. Only after a while did she come and sit down next to me. She reached out, held my hand and said only, "I like you." I responded, "I like you too."

I realized that the situation with Monica had turned more complicated. Monica had no control whatsoever about her eating habits. I talked to Bozena and mentioned my observation, which was that after dinner, Monica went to the kitchen, finished all leftovers, such as two pieces of pot roast and potatoes. Then, after that, she had a bowl of ice cream.

Bozena's answer was, "I don't know anymore what to do." I only could answer, "You missed the time to teach her to control herself."

Because Monica had Down Syndrom, Bozena and Bartek spoiled her from an early age on and missed the chance to teach her how to control herself and prepare for her future. Monica refused to keep Monica in the special school. Finally, Bozena and Bartek arranged to homes-school Monica in reading and writing. Monica has developed handcrafting skills, and hopefully, she will be able to use them and support herself.

I was sad when I left Bozena. I felt that she didn't deserve that heavy burden. My impression was that both she and Bartek had aged mentally. There were no smiles on their faces, and no sign of hope for improvement. I really missed the laughing and joking that we had always shared.

Part Three
Start of a Better and Happier Life

Chapter 19
Chicago Part One
You Must Love the City

Never ever in my life had I ever considered going to the United States. My dream was to immigrate either to Canada or Australia. Somehow, nothing drew me to the States, even though I visited my sister in Chicago in 1971, and I visited my school friend after sixteen years briefly in New Jersey. At that time I had the chance to see briefly New York City.

Due to the spy affair in the West German Embassy in Warsaw, my friend and co-worker Barbara and I were transferred. It all happened overnight at the end of the year 1973. Our Ambassador and the Foreign Office in Bonn wanted to avoid any conflicts with the Polish Secret Service. They would have tried to obtain secret information from us.

The only message we received was that Barbara had been transferred to Brussels and me to Chicago. Still, we both had to return to the main office in Bonn for further training. I had to pass an exam in English, and Barbara in the French language. In addition, my car had to be converted to U.S. standards, such as different tires, light adjustments and a few other little items.

In Bonn, I rented a small room on monthly basis with the availability to cancel it at any time when my deployment to the U.S. was announced. My household items, which were packed in a container in Warsaw, had arrived in Bonn, and were ready to be shipped to Chicago. Before departing, my car had to be containerized and secured for shipping.

I arrived in Chicago on February 14, 1974. At the airport I was picked up by a member of the Consulate General. For four weeks I stayed in one of the oldest hotels near Lincoln Park until I found an apartment in a high-rise building. I was informed about the neighborhoods, and warned about those which were not safe.

On Sheridan Road, a parallel street to the Lake Shore Drive, several high-rise buildings had vacancies. I chose one that had just been built.

This building had a triangular shape, fifty-five floors, a fitness center, shopping possibilities, and a doctor's office. To park the car I could use either the underground garage for a monthly fee, or park outside the building, which was fenced and secure. The house was guarded by a doorman and codes were assigned for each apartment for security reasons. I selected a one-bedroom apartment in the ninth floor with a view of Lake Michigan. In the morning, I could watch the sunrise from my bed. I felt very secure. I hardly used my car because bus transportation was convenient. The bus stop was in front of our building, and at each side street along Michigan Avenue. The Consulate General was located at the corner of Michigan Avenue and Monroe Street in downtown Chicago. The drive from my home to work took about fifteen minutes, depending on the traffic, and only if the Michigan Avenue Bridge wasn't raised in order to let sailboats pass from the Chicago River to Lake Michigan.

I learned fairly quickly how to commute to and from work. Co-workers were very helpful. They showed me around, explained shopping areas, and mentioned cultural events.

I was told that the work term for the Consulate General would last two years. Knowing that, I was eager to see and learn as much as I could, not only about the city, but the country as well. Chicago is located in the Midwest, and is a city for everyone, no matter what nationality. Chicago has many ethnic groups, including Polish, Irish, Mexican, Portuguese and many more.

In mid-1974, we experienced a recession, which was difficult for everybody. I remember that gas stations were open only for four hours a day, depending on the available supply. At that time, my fiancé, Stanley, arrived, and I tried very much to find a job for him. He was an engineer in the computer field. Unfortunately, he had no knowledge of the English language and I was new in the city and country. At that time, I did not know how to approach companies, send out resumes or contact companies on the phone. Due to a close friendship with a German couple, I was able to find a job for him in a lamp factory. It was not easy for him to start working at the lowest level, but there was no choice. It was necessary to apply for a work permit for Stanley, which we received after short period of time. In July of that year we got married.

Shortly after that we filled for permanent residency. My sister Karin was willing to be our sponsor. Stanley slowly worked his way up to be the foreman in the company. His salary was pretty low and we had to budget our money. Stanley had to learn how to get around without knowing the language, pass the driver's license test and be responsible in regard to spending money. This he never learned.

The winter of 1974 was pretty tough. Chicago is known as the Windy City, and this has to be experienced. It was December when a snowstorm hit. While being at work and looking out of the office window, we realized how heavy the snow was coming down. By early afternoon we all were sent home. We thought we could fight the traffic, but how wrong we were. As I mentioned before, usually it took me fifteen minutes to get home. This time, I sat on the bus for three hours. The bus driver tried all kinds of tricks to go around stranded cars. He drove over the grass in parks, but nothing helped. In the bus, people were very polite to each other since we all were in the same situation. People alternately offered up their seats because of the long stop-and-go drive. Finally, after three hours, the bus arrived at the corner of Foster and Sheridan Road. Here the driver announced that this was as far as he could go. The distance to the high-rise building where I lived was approximately five hundred yards. By the time we arrived there, the snow was blown high and the wind was very strong. We needed strong men to help us through the wind and into the building.

I was finally home. Next morning when I looked out of the window I saw so many cars stuck in the snow and ice on Lake Shore Drive. Nothing was moving. Hardly anyone could get to work. As quick as the snow storm came in, the same way it disappeared. The city maintenance crews made sure that the traffic started to roll again.

By the end of 1975, I was told that my working term at the Consulate was completed and that I was supposed to be transferred to Liverpool in the UK. For a year I had kept my marriage to a Polish citizen as secret as possible. Nobody in the Consulate General knew about it. Here I knew it was the opportunity to resign from diplomatic employment. I stated that I had just married and would like to remain in the U.S. The resignation was accepted.

During the two years in Chicago, I met people from the German American Chamber of Commerce. The Consulate General and the German American Chamber of Commerce had a very close working relationship. They were also located in the same building, but on different floors. I contacted and informed them about my decision to remain in Chicago. Mr. Neal, the president of the Chamber of Commerce, was delighted and informed me about openings for a bilingual secretary position at a machine tool company called Battenfeld. This company originated from Germany and was established in Skokie, Illinois, a suburb on Chicago's northern border.

They offered service and spare parts for injection molding machines that were sold in North America.

I was introduced to Mrs. Flindt, the president of the company, who hired me following the first interview. I was assigned to the spare parts and service department. The manager of this department was Mr. Stark, who also originated from Germany, but had lived in the U.S. for couple of years. I loved my job as a bilingual secretary. I attended machine tool shows at the McCormick Place convention center and met many interesting people.

Life also started to improve for my husband. We enjoyed being with friends, discovered new restaurants, went together to theaters, music halls, movies and entertained each other on several occasions.

After four years in the high-rise building on Lake Shore Drive, we decided to purchase a house in Skokie. It was a twenty-five year-old, two-story house with three bedrooms, two bathrooms, a living and dining room, an old-fashioned kitchen and a basement consisting of one small room for the furnace and appliances, and a bigger room for storage. From the basement we could exit to the backyard. We were aware that we needed to remodel, not only the kitchen, but also the bathrooms and make the basement useful.

A Polish friend, Mike Biedron, who was a builder in Indiana, helped us to redo the kitchen. We ordered new cabinets, a sink, stove and refrigerator. Prior to delivery of these items, Mike and I put tiles on the wall and the floor. We installed a counter which divided the kitchen from the dining room, and which also served as breakfast counter.

When the kitchen was done, my next remodeling project was one of the bathrooms. The second followed later. The only help I needed from outside was to install a new toilet and sink. The wall needed tiles around the bathtub, which was the hardest work. Here I discovered that the drywall was moist. I asked a co-worker for help. He knew how to handle plumbing.

At first we had to cut out the moist drywall, replace some pipes and fittings and close it again with a piece of drywall. When it was dry, I sanded it and continued with the tiles. My hands were already sore and partially cut. Since money was tight, I had no choice but to continue the work by myself. Stanley did not show any support. He did not even know how to handle tools. I had learned to be handy during an earlier relationship, and had my own little toolbox. The repair of the second bathroom was even tougher. The walls were uneven and inclined. I worked on that partially through the night. But I made it and was proud about this achievement. I was glad to have been able to do such work and that I had also saved a lot of money. The house started to be warm and cozy.

A Doberman puppy joined us. We called him Nero, and he grew to be my protector. Unfortunately, the breeder did not do a good job raising the dog. Nero was hyper and difficult to handle. We were forced to have a six-foot fence around our property and muzzle him when walking him down the street. No male person was allowed to come near me. Even my sister was scared to be around the dog. I sent him to obedience school, but it did not do any good. He listened just to my commands. However, as soon as somebody else was around, he seemed to be more aggressive. Later, when Stanley and I got divorced, the dog got sick and had to be put down. He was only five years old.

I stayed with the Battenfeld Company for four years. In late 1979 I was hired away by another German American company, called American Pfauter. My occupation was purchasing agent, which gave me a wide range of responsibility. We had a wonderful working atmosphere.

On weekends we had picnics and played volleyball. Twice a year we arranged an open house, specifically during the International Machine Tool Show. The company ordered limo service and invited customers to our facility for beer and bratwurst. I knew the machines which we produced and assembled very well. Our engineering department taught me all the details, and how to read the drawings.

Unfortunately, in 1983, the economy was at its worst. Together with seven other co-workers, I had to leave the company and search for another job. The biggest shock for me was to go to the unemployment office in order to apply for unemployment payments.

I was surrounded by people of Latin descent. When I presented my German passport and the green card, I got the impression that the person at the counter had seen it probably for the first time. She was confused. The result was that I received my payments after two long months.

While searching continuously, I was invited by eleven companies for job interviews. I also had sent out thirty-two resumes, but I was either overqualified, or the jobs didn't pay enough. In desperation, I started my own home-cleaning business. In addition, I got a part-time job at the Sears headquarters through an employment agency, and I also joined a translation office. In other words, I worked three different jobs. My day started at seven in the morning and ended at eleven at night. At least this work could cover the incoming bills. Still, I spread the word around, specifically through the Chamber of Commerce, that I was looking for steady employment. I was lucky when I received a call from Canada and learned that the company Kloeckner was moving to the Chicago area and I was offered a job as bilingual secretary. The salary was not the greatest, but at least I was back on regular-hour terms. The Kloeckner company represented one line of tool machines for the Germany company Scharmann. We shared the same building in Carol Stream, a western suburb of Chicago.

The business started to pick up, and in 1984, Scharmann dropped the Kloeckner line.

My co-worker David Harcourt and I were now employees of Scharmann. Besides the hard work, everything looked brighter. I was assigned to the Manhattan Project at the Pontiac facility in Michigan as a coordinator between German and American engineers. They were trying to build a one-piece engine cylinder head and block.

The duration of this project took over six months, and I was commuting between Chicago and Detroit on weekends. It was a great experience. I learned to balance the different mentalities within the German and American members of the team. Later, I was described as the mother of the team.

Often, I had to listen to peoples' personal problems, how they missed their spouses and other difficulties they had with the company. But there was also fun involved.

In 1984, after ten years of marriage, I decided to get divorced. It was a constant struggle and an irreconcilable situation. My efforts to convince Stanley to adjust and accept the American lifestyle and learn English did not succeed. I suggested, or even begged him, to participate in evening school and learn technical terminology, which he needed in his working field. In addition, I asked him to eliminate connections to people who had a bad influence on him. That did not mean to lose old friends. Polish people who were around him gave me the impression that they were homesick, and they were constantly whining. I asked him to look at the future in a positive way. We used to have nice parties and gatherings, and the people we knew had come to the U.S. to build new and better lives for themselves. This eventually happened. One couple started an auto dealership in Indianapolis, another couple went to evening classes and learned to be successful lawyers, and another couple got involved in business. At the end, everybody was doing very well.

In 1984, following our divorce, I decided to apply for American citizenship. I had been in America for ten years, and I felt very comfortable. People were very good to me and I did not have any negative experiences. I took this step knowing that I would not return for good to Germany, only to visit my family. At the end of October 1984, I finally received my citizenship papers.

Work continued to be positive, and I enjoyed concerts, the opera house, and in the summertime, I loved to go downtown to meet with friends in a cafe or for dinner. On weekends, I played tennis with co-workers. After I met Rudi, my future husband, it was even more fun to explore new places and to travel through the country.

We bought a town home in Glendale Heights. We were joined by a Standard Schnauzer puppy, which we called Coco. Rudi and I married in July 1987. We met through our company, where Rudi worked as a senior service engineer. Prior to our marriage, we dated for a year. Since he was traveling a lot, he asked me to check on his mail and pay the incoming bills with the signed checks he left behind. We developed a trustful relationship.

In 1991, our company transferred us to Germany, and it was the most difficult decision for me to leave Chicago and the U.S. The decision to go to Germany was based on a request by the headquarters. Rudi was needed, and the manpower capacity at the company's Chicago facility was shrinking. On the other hand, Rudi did not get enough back-up from his supervisor in regard to the retrofits of older machines, so the working atmosphere was not good. When we left, we did not know whether or when we would ever come back. I had lived over seventeen years in the U.S. and had gotten used to the lifestyle and the wide landscape. Germany is small compared to the U.S.

Suddenly I discovered that I did not fit in anymore. I had the feeling that people in Germany had changed over the years. The truth was that they hadn't changed, I had. It was a different environment. I got the impression that the people had forgotten to be friendly. In the little town where we ended up, I tried to teach people how to say a friendly Guten Tag, or Gruess Got, which was the usual greeting. I also taught them to pick up the poop from their dogs. It was funny to see the spectators when the twenty-foot container arrived with our household. This was something very new to them. It was the same spectacle when we left after five years to return to the U.S. There was nothing that appealed to me in Germany, and I became very homesick. The only pleasant events were visiting the city of Ulm or Munich and the Black Forest.

Finally, a friend from Wisconsin, Ron Engelke, brought us back to the U.S. He also employed us in his company and we stayed there for four years. We lived in Germantown and worked in Menomonee Falls.

The life and work up north was enjoyable, however, Chicago was always on my mind. We stayed in touch with some previous Scharmann co-workers and friends whom we visited frequently. Then one day we received a call from Scharmann and we were asked to rejoin the company, but in the meantime, the company had relocated from Chicago to Cincinnati. We did not hesitate to take this step. After a meeting with the manager, and after listening to his offer, we accepted it and moved our household from Wisconsin. There was not much time to prepare for this move. First we needed to sell our house. We called two realtors. One of them sold our house within two days.

In May 2001, we found a home outside Cincinnati, in Loveland, which is called the Sweetheart of Ohio. Here we stayed until we retired and moved to New Mexico.

We often think about Chicago. We used to visit Downtown restaurants, sit outside and watch people go by. We took boat rides on the Chicago River and Lake Michigan. Most of all, I miss the shopping in Chicago. We also loved to show our visitors around who enjoyed the big city flair.

Chapter 20
Chicago Part Two - Stanley Pisz

In May 2011, while visiting Poland, I scheduled a visit to the cemetery Powazki, where Stanley was buried in October 2010. I was informed about Stanley's passing by a former lady friend, Mrs. Nowakowska. We talked on the phone few times, and I promised to be in touch with her when I would be in Warsaw.

I met Mrs. Jadwiga Nowakowska (she calls herself Iga), on May 10, 2011, while I was visiting Warsaw. I had never met her and had no knowledge of her existence. In our phone conversations prior to meeting, she tried to explain to me her relationship with Stanley and how much she had helped him during his last days and how she felt betrayed by him, especially by his friends, who were after his money. They had given her a hard time.

Apparently, a few days prior to his death, a last will had been issued with her being named as the only beneficiary. This never was accepted and executed, and she wound up fighting with his closest friends over that matter. The only money she obtained was that to cover the funeral and memorial service. Mrs. N. complained that as long as Stanley was in the hospital, not one of those friends even bothered to visit him. That's nothing unusual in my opinion. However, I do not know the relationship Stanley had with his friend Roman.

Ordinary Woman

I listened to Mrs. N's. story in which she told me that she had met Stanley upon his return from the U.S. to Poland in 2003, and that they had been close for a few years. Mrs. N. accompanied him in 2004 to Florida and other places, but she always covered her own expenses. Stanley, as I knew him well, was never generous. I describe such behavior as being a taker, but never a giver. Their relationship was on and off. Stanley was a restless and choosy person. He started several other relationships, but after a short period of time dropped the ladies and again returned to Mrs. N., who was good enough to be his chauffeur to and from the hospital. Apparently, she did not mind, and cared for him until he passed away.

The following obituary was placed in the paper (translated):

"On October 5, 2010, Stanisław Pisz passed away. The burial will follow the arranged Memorial Service at the St. Karol Boromeusz church on the date of October 11 at 10.00 a.m. Location is the cemetery Old Powązki. Rest in peace, dear Stasiu. In deep sorrow, Iga."

In spite of all the ups and downs in this relationship, Mrs. N. was very emotional, and she visits his burial place regularly. Each time, she lights a candle for him and keeps him in her prayers.

While visiting his grave at the cemetery, I hoped to find some closure and put the past with Stanley to rest. Here, however, all the wounds surfaced. I have never opened up to anyone about the ten years of having been married to Stanley. Indeed, it was a bittersweet relationship which started while I was on an assignment in Warsaw in 1972.

As one of the embassy employees, I felt the need to get in contact with other foreigners. On one occasion, I had the opportunity to visit the United States Embassy. I knew it had a lounge and a bar. The friendly atmosphere helped me to get acquainted with its employees and visitors from the U.S. I met the director of Pan American Airways who was stationed in

Warsaw and whose family used to live in Kenosha, Wisconsin. Ignacy, which was his name, had several Polish friends whom I met occasionally at his home parties. One of his friends, a lady called Bozena, my best girlfriend, was one of the guests in Ignacy's house who knew Stanley Pisz. During a conversation with Stanley, Bozena mentioned my name and suggested that she was willing to introduce him to me. This happened, and Stanley invited me to a cafe where we could talk and get acquainted. We saw each other as often as my work schedule allowed. He was very polite and we became closer. His father was a teacher in Tarnow, but had passed away several years earlier. His mother lived alone in the city. On one occasion we drove to Tarnow so I could meet his mom, a very sweet and nice lady. I knew that mother and son loved and respected each other, however, I did wonder that he did not visit her more often.

As time went by, he proposed to me and we started to talk about our future. In the meantime, I became aware that I had to leave the country very suddenly. I received the news that I was to be transferred to the Consulate General in Chicago for two years. Of course, this started to be a burden on our relationship because of the distance between Poland and America. We talked about how to deal with such a separation. I asked him to start learning English because I intended to invite him to Chicago, and then we could decide whether to live in Poland, America, or even Germany.

Before leaving for Chicago, I stayed in Bonn for three months, passed the English language test and receive training about the tasks involved for the position I was to be placed. Several times a week I called Stanley in Warsaw, and later, from Chicago. When I was asked him if he was in the process of learning English, he always answered with a "yes." This was one of the big lies which I experienced throughout our marriage.

He also did not tell me that he had started the efforts to come to the States. Later, he confessed that he had been invited to the Polish Security Police for interrogation sessions. It was known that we were engaged, and he was asked to spy on me, my co-workers and other Polish citizens who had left the country. Also, he was asked to return after thirty days.

But Stanley had other plans. He confided his plans to a friend, Roman. He was supposed to sell the condominium in Warsaw and distribute all the furniture. This had to be done secretly to avoid suspicion and jeopardize his travel plans. Roman was Stanley's closest friend. After this arrangement, Stanley got his visa and purchased a round-trip ticket. Up to then, everything had gone smoothly. He flew via Pan American Airways, and Ignacy, his friend, did not miss to present him on the plane with a double glass of cognac, wishing him a safe trip.

Stanley arrived in Chicago in June of 1974. At that time I had a one-bedroom apartment on the ninth floor in a fifty-five-story high-rise on Sheridan Road with a wonderful view of Lake Michigan.

When Stanley arrived, he started to pressure me to get married. I was hesitant and not sure, since we did not know each other too well. But he insisted and we married on my birthday on July 31, 1974. This marriage had to be kept secret due to the rules that a consulate employee of one of the western countries was not allowed to be married to a citizen of a communist country. This, unfortunately, applied to us.

From that moment on the dilemma in our marriage started. First of all, Stanley admitted that he did not participate in English courses and, therefore, could not communicate with people. This also resulted in a terrible jealousy. Whenever I came home he searched my purses and wanted explanations in regard to business cards that had been given to me.

In 1974, the recession made it difficult to find a job for Stanley. I remember being forced to sell my car (BMW), which

I had brought from Germany, because I did not trust Stanley to drive it due to his lack of experience. We then purchased a Pontiac Trans Am, and sure enough, he was involved in an accident. There was a good outcome thanks to a policeman who himself was Polish. Finally, I found a job for Stanley in a lighting factory through a friend, and I was glad to see him busy and earning money. But this was not enough by all means. Prior to that we had applied for permanent residency, and my sister was our sponsor. Even though we had to wait for an interview and approval, a temporary working permit was issued. I have to mention that the favor my sister granted after we had been reunited and had solved our differences after seven years of silence. My sister and brother-in-law did not have the best opinion about Stanley, especially after he badmouthed me to them and complained that I had to buy food with a credit card. He never explained to them that we were struggling financially.

Stanley developed into a show off man. He never put a hand on items to be repaired and forbade me to mention that he was working in a factory sweeping floors. He also threatened that if I did not do whatever he thought was right, he would go to the Consul General and report that we were married. This would have had consequences with regard to my employment situation. I was finally relieved when my term at the consulate came to an end and I was supposed to be transferred to Liverpool, UK. I took the chance to resign with the argument that I had just married and would remain in the U.S. My employer, the Ministry of Foreign Affairs in Germany, understood, but still offered to move my household back to Germany in case I changed my mind.

We had moved from the Lake Shore apartment to a house in Skokie. At this time, many people of Polish background had come to Chicago, and soon, we have built up connections and friendships with them. Everybody started a new life, taking any possible work which was offered. We did many things together. We organized parties, went together to movies or theaters, and in the summer, met at the pool.

This changed very quickly. Most of them were eager to achieve their lifestyle goals first and started to show off either with cars, homes, furs and finally, extended families, including their babies. One of them was Stanley. Our standard Pontiac Trans Am was not good enough for him anymore. Therefore, he purchased the advanced model on credit. Our money fights got worse. I took an additional job and cleaned homes together with one or two Polish ladies, and also worked at night in a translation office. It was important for me to pay the incoming bills and also to reimburse a builder who had installed a new kitchen in our home

The builder showed me how to remodel two bathrooms with tiles, scrape off old paint from the windows and repaint them, and many other little tasks. My hands were sore and cut, and sometimes I asked a co-worker to help me with replacing the drywall. I did wood paneling in the basement and installed a bar counter all by myself. While I was scraping paint and pounding nails, Stanley sat there with his pipe and watched with amazement. Only at the very end did he offer to help. I had to teach him how to handle a drill after he damaged the wall with holes while installing a shelf. Only later on did he pick up on some handyman tasks, and only after I got very sick due to his threats and abuse. I had to stay in the hospital for two weeks, five days of which were in intensive care. Following surgery, I spent two weeks at home recovering. I lost two thirds of my stomach because of ulcers.

The company I worked for was generous enough to pay me for the whole month of not being at work. All my co-workers cared for me and knew about the problems; therefore, they invited me to join them occasionally for social events: summer concerts in Ravinia Park outside of Chicago. This most beautiful setting and atmosphere helped me to forget the dark side of my daily life. It was also a surprise to meet the Duke Ellington Orchestra during one of these events. All the members recognized me from the time we had met in 1971 in Leningrad.

Here again, Stanley accused me of having affairs with my co-workers. This brought me to the point to accept an invitation to New York to visit friends I knew from one of my trips to the Bahamas. I used the excuse that this was a business trip. I had to get away from Stanley.

Stanley did not at all understand. He did not have any feelings for others, not even for me. We had no sex life during all those years, which just drove me away from him. I felt like a cleaning mate who did the cooking, worked all day and had to entertain his friends. He was a "shining party person." I never complained to anyone, but when the time came, I had to put a stop to things. From a certain time on, I refused to host those people who only recollected the good times in Poland and complained about everything in the States.

Finally, I told them to pack and return to that wonderful country. At that time, Poland had many restrictions set by the Communist regime. Only few of these friends eventually returned to Poland, and so did Stanley.

In 1984, Stanley shared with friends that he had married me only for material and financial reasons. At that point I knew that it was time to go. I packed my personal items, took the used car, which was almost falling apart, and left. The company helped me find a small apartment which I later shared with a co-worker until I could afford it myself. Stanley and I agreed to file for divorce. The house remained in Stanley's possession; however, he had to pay back the amount which I had invested at the time of purchase. He paid me in partial payments. Our divorce was finalized later in the year.

From our common friends I learned that Stanley had married a lady of Polish descent, but this relationship did not work out for either. Later, he was socializing with a circle of Russian ladies, again with no success. Whenever Stanley faced a difficult time, or if he was in a need, he would call me asking for help. He almost lost the house, and here again, I, as a softhearted person, helped him to pay the monthly mortgage.

While I was working at a German machine tool company I met Rudi and we married in 1987. Stanley knew about it, but had trouble accepting it. Friends told him that he had made a big mistake to treat me the way he did. The first time I saw him in tears was when Rudi and I left for business to Germany 1991. At that time, he had lost his job and asked me to help him with a resume in order to find a job. However, he never did the resume, and started to be a cab driver. This apparently kept him above water financially and he could cover his bills.

In 2003, after he had sold the house in Skokie, Stanley decided to return to Poland. I lost contact to him for several years. Only in 2009, when I received birthday greetings from him, and with the help of Skype, did I have the chance to see and hear him again. At that time, he told me about his illness and treatments for colon cancer. The rest is history, as I learned it at the cemetery in May, 2011.

Chapter 21
People to be Remembered

For many years while traveling or being on assignments, famous people crossed my path who are worth mentioning. Quite often I saw a prominent person at the airport, or even on the plane. But mostly I remember people whom I always admired. Therefore I like to focus strongly on those people.

In Moscow and Leningrad, while working as a tourist guide in 1970, I was introduced to members of the Bolshoi and Kirov Theater (today it is renamed in Mariinsky Opera and Ballet Theater). There were singers, dancers and musicians whom I met. I felt very comfortable among them. As a child my mother encouraged me to take ballet lessons and play the piano, but, after the war money was short and we could not afford to pay for the lessons. I never lost my interest in music and theater.

During my two months duty in Leningrad I stayed in the old Hotel Europe, which had a proud history hosting many famous people. The hotel is located on Nevsky Prospekt, the main street of Leningrad, making it an ideal place from which to visit the city's main sights and attractions.

Duke Ellington and his orchestra stayed here while performing on several evenings in the concert hall. We met in the hotel lobby and restaurant and got acquainted. Duke occupied one of the suites, and the hotel furnished him with a white grand piano. He told me that he did not need much sleep and, therefore, he played and composed at night. His son, Mercer, was managing him and also made sure that the proper food, such as steaks, was flown in from the States.

I got friendly with Harry Carney, a saxophone player, with whom I enjoyed walking on the Neva riverbanks. At that time my English was not as good and Harry would laugh about my saying, "Let's go by foot" instead of, "Let's walk." Everybody, including Duke, was very charming and fun to be with. I saw them all later in 1970 in Germany when they arrived at the Dusseldorf Airport.

I still remember Duke wearing a white warm coat with two missing buttons. The orchestra was performing in Dortmund, and then they continued their tour through thirty-five cities before covering the Far East countries.

When I arrived in Chicago in 1974 for the scheduled work term at the German Consulate General, I learned that Duke Ellington had passed away on May 27th. I watched the funeral on TV. Ella Fitzgerald stood up and sang Solitude, the old funeral hymn from New Orleans. The Ellington era had come to an end, but his legacy will remain.

In late summer, Mercer Ellington brought the orchestra to Chicago and I attended the concert in Ravinia Park. During the intermission I approached the stage. Harry Carney saw me and said, "I can't believe it, that's you, Irmgard Bothmer!" and we embraced and exchanged a few words. A few months later I learned about his death.

As a member of the German Consulate General following a term completion at the German Embassy in Warsaw, I found many occasions to meet various important and interesting people. It is known that embassies and consulates represent the home country and arrange political, economic and cultural meetings and parties in order to get acquainted with those of other countries. I had the chance to meet the former president of the Federal Republic of Germany, Walter Sheel, and his wife Mildred, a doctor of radiology who was very involved in finding a cure for cancer. Unfortunately, several years later she lost her own fight with cancer.

Many other visits with politicians followed. Our Cultural Department was responsible for guests who were invited to perform in the U.S. Among them was the conductor Herbert von Karajan with the Berlin Philharmonic Orchestra.

Herbert von Karajan was born in Salzburg, Austria. He was known as a controversial person due to the fact that he had been a member of the Nazi Party. He conducted at the Staedtisches Theater in Ulm after the War. In 1955 he was made principal conductor of the Berlin Philharmonic and was associated with it until his resignation in 1989. Herbert von Karajan was known as being very strict, but he was also loved. He helped young talents to develop their abilities and led them to fame.

Mr. Karajan was invited to perform in Chicago by Sir George Solti, director of the Chicago Symphony Orchestra. Our Consulate made sure that we got tickets for the evening and the post-concert cocktail party.

On that evening I was sitting in the first row, which is not the best sitting for a concert. To enjoy the sound and acoustics, it is best to be seated further back, away from the stage. However, I was glad to be seated so close to the stage and observe the maestro. It was known that he had back problems and all his movements were accompanied by pain. The Symphony employees, therefore, installed a guarding around the pedestal which served as support and secured him while conducting.

I was amazed at his personality, his control over the orchestra and ability to conduct without the use of notebooks. His eyes were closed through the whole concert; his arms hardly moved, and there was kind of softness.

Mr. Karajan attended the cocktail party only briefly, which was understandable, but he did not miss to greet everyone present. Sir George Solti accompanied him back to the hotel.

We all were very impressed and grateful to have met this maestro.

Another guest performer invited to the Chicago music hall was a baritone singer, Dietrich Fischer-Dieskau. He was born in Berlin, studied and made his professional debut in Freiburg in 1947, and joined the Berlin Municipal Opera as its principal baritone. He became one of the foremost interpreters of the German Lieder, particularly the song cycle of the composer Franz Schubert. Mr. Fischer-Dieskau was a very handsome gentleman, and again we had the pleasure to meet him in person following his concert.

The Chicago Opera House was very important to me while living in the city. It was known to have excellent performers, and to be very particular in choosing them. Since I was one of the donating members of this opera, we were invited for cocktails and got a tour through the house. We learned about performers who were welcome or not welcome to return. One of those performers was Luciano Pavarotti. Several times he did not keep his schedule and/or was late, and his demands were outrageous.

On the contrary, Placido Domingo was a welcomed guest. I remember the evening when I was invited to the opening performance of the opera Carmen by Bizet. This was my first opportunity to see Mr. Domingo live. I was overwhelmed by his voice and performance, and since then I've been an avid fan.

Compared to other artists, Placido Domingo stands out as a person without any scandals. He was committed to his family, but even more to his work. He organized fundraisers for people in need, such as earthquake survivors in Mexico. I had the chance to be at another of his performances in Verona, Italy. The excellence of each performance made him worldwide famous as a singer, conductor, and teacher of young talents.

I feel privileged and happy having met these talented people. Wonderful memories will remain forever.

Chapter 22
Blind Date – Meet the Con Man

In 1986, approximately, two years after my divorce from Stanley Pisz after ten years of marriage, it was time to start socializing and meet new people. It was supposed to be a new start after all the disappointments.

A longtime acquaintance, Mike and his wife Terry, whom I had known since 1971, called me one day and encouraged me to start dating.

"That's great," I answered, "but where do I meet someone interesting?"

"A business friend from England is in town and I told him a lot about you. I will be glad to set up a meeting place for you two," said Mike. He then described and suggested a restaurant and gave me the name of the person I was supposed to meet. It was Kenneth Senior from Manchester, UK.

I arrived and met Ken, who was already there. Visually it was obvious that he came from England due to his reddish hair, lots of freckles and unhealthy complexion.

The dinner date went well, and we had a nice conversation. I liked his humor and we decided to meet again. His time was restricted due to shows or exhibitions either in Chicago or Atlanta.

Ken arranged to be in Chicago frequently. We spent as much time together as was possible. I knew that he was married to a Dutch lady, Thea, but there had been, according to his statements, some conflict in the marriage. He told me that besides living in Manchester he was commuting to Northampton where his work place was located. He left home on Monday's and returned on Friday's or Saturday's each week. During the week he rented a room at a bed and breakfast. He told me about his son Peter, whom he adored, but who did not have a good relationship with his mother. Little by little I learned a bit more and heard different stories. At that particular time, I did not bother to search for details; I rather wanted to spend some time and have relaxing moments. So we drove to one of the resorts in Wisconsin during the winter and spent a relaxing weekend there.

For the first time during dinner I realized that he had trouble with his teeth. He then told me that he had loose teeth and asked one time for Super Glue in order to hold the teeth in place. When I asked him why he didn't see a dentist, he only mentioned a lack of money.

This was repeated several times and he explained how little he earned as sales person and how the company made no travel money available. I paid for the hotel and meals. We had separate rooms because I was not ready for a sexual encounter. Whether he told me the truth or not, I was not sure. He used to mention the phrase, "Eventually I will pay you back." I believed him and let it go.

I was assigned as a coordinator for a project between our company and Pontiac/GM and had to travel with some engineers to Europe (Germany and France) in order to visit machine tool companies which would be chosen as suppliers for our project. In Paris we visited Citroen. On the only free weekend I had, I planned to go to London and meet Ken. He made a hotel reservation, which I paid. He showed me some of London, but not much due to street closures for an international marathon. The only attraction I remember seeing was the Windsor Castle.

It was time to return to Paris for continuous meetings. The next time I saw Ken in Germany. He picked me up at the airport in Cologne. He was on a business trip from England to Germany and the Netherlands where he had to visit customers. I was even introduced to his business friends as his steady companion. During this trip he told me another story about his wife Thea. She was unstable mentally and under heavy medication, and while he was gone a nurse was assigned to watch her during the daytime.

He also mentioned to me that several years prior he had had testicular cancer and lost part of his genitals and, therefore, had lost his sex drive. Great, I thought, because I was not eager to have sex anyhow. More and more I got aggravated when he was discussing and comparing the British and American language.

When I returned to the States, I noticed that he never called me. And it was strange that he rather waited for my calls. Still, I did not get suspicious until he came to the States on business and asked me for money. He told me was that his wife had breast cancer and he was not able to cover the costs of the medication.

Again he told me, "Eventually I will pay you back." Me, the stupid and believing person, gave him five hundred dollars. I am still waiting for that money.

Neither telephone calls nor letters were directed to me. Because in one way I liked him, I was worried sick and turned to my friend Mike for advice.

His secretary called me with the message that Ken would be in town shortly and that a private meeting for me with him would be set up. I was trembling and angry when I drove to the meeting. He had no excuse or explanation as to why he had cut off the communication with me. I asked him, "Are all the stories about the health of your wife true?" and, "Is it true that your company is not paying you enough for you to get around?" He answered:

"Partially yes, but I could not leave my wife, I would not get any divorce due to her mental illness."

My last question was, "Did you get involved with me for a good time on my expense?" Here again he answered, "Eventually you will get it back." The secretary whom I asked to attend this meeting stood up, opened the door and asked him to leave. Since then I have never heard from him. A business acquaintance in London found out in 2004 that Ken had moved from Manchester to Northampton, but that was all I knew. Whether his wife moved with him or passed away in the meantime, I don't know.

Chapter 23
Successful Marriage/Relationship
A Tribute to my Husband Rudi

At the heart of every successful relationship is respect. In case you are wondering about love and trust and all those other important ingredients of a good relationship, the more we think about it the more we realize that without respect a good relationship cannot exist. If we truly love someone, we do not lie to them or hurt their feelings. One has to experience good and bad things over the years until we finally realize that there is happiness in the world and that we just need to open our eyes and hearts.

After two failed marriages I almost gave up the search for my soul mate. After five years of marriage to K. H. Bettels, which was filled with verbal and physical abuse, I decided to cut the strings and get divorced. This marriage was later annulled in 1967. My second try with Stanley lasted ten years. The marriage was built on lies and dishonesty. When I divorced in 1984 and lost confidence in relationships, my work filled the gap.

But then it happened in 1986 in the Chicago area. The international company headquartered in Germany for which I worked requested skilled people to come from overseas. Usually their work tasks were for a short period of time, but some signed up for an annual contract. These were engineers and technicians involved in highly sophisticated projects. I answered phone calls, passed information or instructions to them which originated from the engineering department. Since customers' sites were located all over the country, there were no opportunities to meet the engineers in person.

I remember when Rudi came to the office. He entered, looked at me and marched straight to the service department. Later on he told me that he asked the boss, "Who is she?" I was new to him. The boss answered, "This is Irma." That was it. I didn't know whether he felt some attraction or interest. During his regular homecoming, based on a two or three weeks-time period, he invited me for a dinner and concert, which I enjoyed very much. I was not ready for a close relationship. The friendship with the Blind Date Con Man had just terminated and I was still recovering emotionally. My stomach was still crunching thinking about all the untrue stories I had been told.

Rudi guessed that I had to overcome some problems, but he never asked any questions during the healing process that made me feel uncomfortable. We saw each other more often, and gathered together with friends or co-workers. He was very trustful and therefore, I was able to check on his apartment during his absence and take care of bills and other matters.

An incident which took place while he was gone proved to me what kind of friend he was. I injured myself while playing tennis, and therefore had my leg heavily bandaged. I needed a car with an automatic transmission in order to drive to work. He lent me his car, a Honda. I still remember what happened on a particular rainy day. I had an apartment on Golf Road. When I pulled out of the parking lot in front of the apartment building, a speeding car which I had not seen rammed me. The crash was immense, I was unable to drive the car, it had to be towed and repaired. I was trembling and was in a state of a shock. In my twenty-seven years of driving I had never had an accident.

I tried to get hold of Rudi in order to report this mishap. Finally he called. His first question was, "Are you hurt?" and, "As long as you are okay, let's worry about the car later." And so it happened. He arranged the repair and filed the insurance claim. I insisted on paying the uncovered balance.

From this time on he was my best friend, and I was his. There were no intimate moments; we both respected each others privacy.

One day, while he was on the road, he called me and announced that he had a surprise for me. But I was allowed to ask only one question per day to find out what kind of surprise it was. I never guessed. Finally, his homecoming was only few days away. By then he advised me to be ready for a trip to Nashville, Tennessee. I was flabbergasted. It turned out to be a wonderful trip. Rudi made double occupancy hotel reservations to make me feel comfortable, and he had the tickets paid for as well. Nashville—home of country music—touched me very much and I learned more about the mentality and culture of the area.

A few months later, Rudi suggested a trip to Canada. Since I had friends in Ontario, I willingly agreed so we could meet them as well. Again, Rudi made all the arrangements. We drove by car and planned to stay overnight in Windsor, Canada.

When we arrived at the hotel there was just one room with two beds available. He felt bad and tried to explain it to me. I agreed to take this room since we had driven several hours and it was late.

Rudi, being very modest, undressed and got ready in the bathroom, while I followed later. Finally, we started to laugh and joke that we were behaving like teenagers and that it was time to break the barriers. From that moment on we never parted. Our relationship developed from a friendship into a love story.

Many wonderful trips we have enjoyed together! We bought a townhome in March, 1987.

Because I was often alone, we decided to get a dog as a companion. Years ago I used to have a Standard Schnauzer, whom I could not take with me from Poland to the U.S. I was missing this lovely dog. Therefore, Rudi and I agreed to search for breeders who had Schnauzers. We found a lady in West Virginia. She got me all information on this breed and I decided to purchase one of her puppies. I had sent her the down payment. Because we were leaving for Hong Kong, we agreed that the dog would be brought to Chicago by a friend and have him available upon our return from Hong Kong. We called the dog Coco. He was just ten weeks old. Coco stayed with us for fifteen years. We buried him in August, 2003.

On the second of July 1987, in order to seal our relationship, I dragged Rudi to the judge (as he always jokes). Nobody was notified or joined us in the marriage ceremony. It was as private as could be. It happened to be the Independence Day weekend, so we took off to St. Louis. Grace, our travel agent, made a reservation in a very old, but cozy, hotel. We got a complementary suite, champagne and flowers. The weather was nice, everything was perfect.

Upon our return we continued with work as usual. Since Rudi was out of town frequently, we took turns; either I flew to him, or he came home. Through those trips with Rudi I learned to love this country. Both our hobbies was photography, therefore, the trips were planned accordingly. Places such as the Yosemite or Yellowstone Park, Death Valley or the battlefields from the Civil War and many other places attracted us. It was wonderful to share these interests, and even compete with each other in a positive way. Rudi encouraged me to go to college in the evening or participate in a sports or health club.

We all have goals in our life; our goal was to overcome several obstacles, such as irregular travel schedules or family differences which could have destroyed our lives. And we did work through the difficult times. We do not miss to say "I love you" whenever there is the chance. We both mean it.

In August 1991 Rudi was transferred back to Germany. We were talking about it quite some time and the decision for me personally to return to Germany after eighteen years was not easy. But I agreed and hoped for the best. To sell the house was one difficulty, and to start from the beginning was another.

I lost track of prices and the lifestyle in Germany, which hit us badly in our pocket book. Most of our savings were spent on a car and decorating a rented, one-hundred-and-twenty-five-year-old home.

Slowly we made new friends and got reacquainted with our family. Rudi does not have any family left; he got along very well with mine. Everybody liked him because of his knowledge and his pleasant attitude. We traveled to Poland to meet my teacher and her families and hosted friends from all over the world. We were called "Pension Pallas" (Bed and breakfast Pallas). We always had, and still have, an open house for friends and family.

For over twenty-five years I have learned who was, and is, my best fried. We both cherish moments of togetherness, whether it is the early cup of coffee in bed or a romantic candlelight dinner. We have never betrayed each other and have never raised our voices, even when we've had differences. At such moments I stop talking and go in seclusion. Usually, Rudi follows me and says something funny so I burst out laughing.

Now that we are a retired couple and are twenty-four hours side-by-side, we had to make some adjustments and keep busy. The volunteer work at school and neighborhood involvements fill our daily hours completely. Since our dog Riley passed away we take the time to include some travelling into our schedule. New Mexico is still quite new to us and there is a lot to be seen. For many years we have directed our interest towards Native American history.

We are also blessed to be in close contact with Rudi's children, and the only grandchild, Alison. Unfortunately, the distances between us and the children are big, but we try to see each other at least once a year.

Chapter 24
In Memory of a Companion
Our Standard Schnauzer Coco

I am a big dog lover. In the past I've had two dogs, a Doberman, and a female Boxer. But during my school time, while I lived in my aunt's household, I took care of my uncle's hunting dog Ari and its puppies. I could not go by without touching and petting dogs wherever I was. I handled them like they were my children, and they loved me because I treated them with love and tenderness. When I was sad or in pain, I coddled and talked to them and they licked my tears away from my face.

During my assignment in Warsaw I purchased a Standard Schnauzer and named him Ferry. It was a beautiful dog whom I showed at the International Dog Show in Poznan when he was a year old. He won first place in his class. I lost Ferry when I was transferred back to Germany and then to Chicago. I did not have the expertise on whether I could bring him to the country, or if special rules applied to have an animal in apartments. Therefore, I asked the breeder to keep him until I was settled. Half a year later I tried to contact the breeder, but I could not find him again. I never forgot Ferry, and I knew that one day I would have a Schnauzer again.

When I met Rudi and we bought a townhome in Glendale Heights, Illinois. Rudi agreed to get a dog. Since Rudi traveled a lot, he knew that I needed a "life creature" to keep me company. I trained the dog and loved him; therefore, I dedicate this chapter to Coco.

August 15, 2003, was a very sad day. Coco, my best companion, friend, or even my child, was never sick before. The day before, he still played with my neighbor Linda. On the fifteenth at five in the morning, he tried to come to me. As usual, he was my alarm-clock. I realized that he could not move his rear legs. I lifted him up, but hardly got a response. He could not stand or even sit. I panicked. Then I called the Kings Veterinary Hospital in Loveland, and because it was early in the morning, I left a message. The nurse responded and asked me to bring the dog in as soon as the doors opened. Coco was checked out and diagnosed with heart failure and stroke. After a short visit to the veterinary hospital, I agreed to put him down, which took place at twelve noon. I stayed with him until the end. I held him in my arms and comforted him while tears were running down my face. And here is how it all began:

Fifteen and half years before, we were searching for Standard Schnauzer breeders. We bought dog magazines and chose several advertisements. I started to call them and tried to get details from the breeders, which were located in different states. Finally I settled on a very nice lady, Patricia Hannum in Virginia. She was kind and sent me all information about the breed line through the Potomac Valley Standard Schnauzer Club. At that time, she had three female puppies and one male. We agreed on the phone that I would send her a down payment of one hundred dollars, and the remaining four hundred we would have available upon delivery. She knew that we would be out of the country at the beginning of March. We then agreed that we would be able to pick-up the puppy on March 30, 1987. At that time, a dog show took place in Chicago, and friends of Ms. Hannum who were showing their dogs were willing to bring the puppy to Chicago. We met them at McCormick Place. The timing was perfect.

Not even resting upon returning from our Hong Kong trip, we rushed to the McCormick Hotel and picked up our puppy. He was a little black bundle and we called him Coco. We were told that he would later turn to his salt-and-pepper color. He was the cutest little fellow with his clipped ears still bandaged in order to make them stand up. From day one he was trained to walk on the leash no matter what kind of weather we had. Of course, his interest was directed to everything that moved. When the wind blew leaves around he tried to catch them.

After a while he got used to the specific timing and he loved his kennel even to the end. It was never a punishment for him to stay in this kennel while we had to go to work. Toys were his friends and they kept him busy. He never chewed on furniture or shoes. His memory and learning ability were extraordinary.

It happened that we were transferred to Germany. When we traveled overseas, Coco accompanied us on the plane. Lufthansa, the German airline, had a special compartment for animals. Coco did well no matter how long the trip took. In Germany he adjusted quickly to his new environment. Friends watched him while we were on vacation, and surprisingly, he adjusted as well to the German language. In other words, he started to be bilingual.

As we trained him from the beginning, he had his special walking time. He liked to play with other dogs his size and even made friends with a Saint Bernard called Caesar.

In Germany, as well in European countries, dogs were allowed in restaurants. Guests never realized that we brought our dog. It was a sure thing for him to be under the table and not bother anyone. People in this little town described him as half human because he seemed to listen and understand. He was funny as well. One anecdote comes to my mind. For three years I was teaching English at the public evening school. Christmas time was around the corner and the semester had come to an end. For the last lesson I planned a little get-together with the students. Everybody participated and brought cookies, juice and other goodies. I also taught the students how to communicate with each other in English. We pretended to be in a restaurant. By the end of the school day I brought home a nicely wrapped cookie box which I left on the kitchen table. Coco never touched anything from the table, whether it was sausage or cheese, but I did not know that he had a sweet tooth.

The next day when I came home I found the little bow and the little Christmas branch which served as a decoration for the box on the floor. Suddenly it dawned on me that the cookie box was missing. I found it under the bench, and looking at it I wondered how he had opened it without any damage. On one side I discovered a little tooth bite, and nothing was ripped. It was opened as gently as it could be. Well, that was not all that happened during that time.

On one of the other evenings a friend of mine drove me home. It was a rainy evening. While unlocking the door, the dog walked toward me and lost his balance. He slipped down the three entrance steps and continued down the driveway. It gave me a terrible scare that he might have been hurt. He was not hurt, and soon enough I learned the reason why he acted that way.

On the second floor we had our living room. On the floor I discovered distributed wrapping papers from chocolate candies which were filled with rum. That was the explanation, Coco was drunk. The result was that he slept through the night snoring loudly. In the morning I had to wake him up. More escapades followed, but none were as drastic as the above.

In 1996 we discovered that he had cancer in his lower jaw, an unusual situation. The veterinary doctor did not treat him properly, and the medication the doctor gave him was too strong. He got weak and vomited blood. We thought he was going to die. Luckily, neighbors informed us about a lady homeopath who treated small animals.

For six months Coco received the proper medication and injections and he recovered slowly. When we got the news by the end of 1996 that we would be transferred back to the U.S., the animal hospital gave Coco another thorough check-up and a clean bill of health.

After that we insisted on an annual check-up with blood counts and X-rays. The results were excellent. Seven years had passed since his cancer experience. Coco acted very normal. He was jumpy, ate properly and slept a little more. He was the most loved and obedient dog and was always welcomed at our friends' homes.

When we had to put him down on August 15, 2003, we requested a cremation. We buried his ashes in the backyard with a rose planted on top of his last resting place.

Grief is the toughest course we sign up for in life. Eventually we got back to normal. Those who loved us helped with silent gestures of support.

After three months of emptiness we got our Riley from the Rescue Association. He was eight years old when we picked him up. He was well trained. We had a lot of fun with this little clown; but often enough I called him Coco instead of Riley. The name Coco will never leave my mind and heart.

Riley stayed with us to his very end as well. He finally lost his vision and hearing. He got weak, and lost control of his bladder. I had to get up at night several times because he was very restless. Finally, on August 8, 2011, I brought him to the animal hospital, where he got the euthanasia injection. He died in my arms being fifteen and a half years old.

Our house is empty again.

Chapter 25
Family Unifications

As it was after World War II and the Korean, Vietnam, Gulf and other wars, many families were torn apart. The International Red Cross and other organizations were, and still are involved in bringing lost, missing and, sad to say, dead family members back home. The search is tremendously hard work, especially if there is not enough information to work with.

It's not just wars, disasters or personal tragedies that cause people to move and get lost around the world. We also do not talk about runaways, as we read about almost every day in the newspapers. I myself was involved in several searches and would like to share the steps and results I experienced.

In 1996 in Germany I met Gisela Wiltfang, the widow of a famous Olympic horse rider. Gerhard Wiltfang was born in April 27, 1946, and suddenly died on July 1, 1997. Mr. Wiltfang was a German equestrian and Olympic champion who won the gold medal for show-jumping at the 1972 Olympic Games in Munich. Further, he won the World Championship in 1978 and the silver medal in 1983.

Mrs. Wiltfang and I met in Thedinghausen while we visited a relative. Over coffee and cake she told me that she might have a sister living in the U.S. The last time she had contact with her sister was in 1974. At that time, the family went through tough times and the children went their own ways.

The only information Mrs. Wiltfang had from her sister was that she had married a U.S. soldier and immigrated to America. The marriage did not last long. She got divorced and remarried. Her last married name was Reid, and her only known residence was in Colorado. Mrs. Wiltfang's wish was to find her sister. She had the feeling that her sister needed some support and help.

When I returned to the States, I did not forget the promise I gave to Mrs. Wiltfang.

Since I did not have much to go with, I wrote several letters to different immigration bureaus. I hoped that the present family name, maiden name, age and approximate date of entering the country would help.

Each of those bureaus responded with the promise to search. But I did not want to wait. I wrote letters to the main Social Security office in Baltimore as well as to the State of Colorado.

I was surprised to find a letter in the mail from the Social Security office stating that Mrs. Reid had been located. I was informed that because of privacy issues they could not give me her address. They suggested that I write a letter to the missing person addressed to the Social Security office which they would forward to Mrs. Reid. Further, they stated that it would be up to Mrs. Reid to respond. It wasn't too long afterward that I got a letter from Mrs. Reid. She seemed to be very happy and thankful. Since then, Mrs. Reid has visited her sister several times in Germany.

At Christmas time in 2004, Mrs. Wiltfang wrote me:

Dear Mrs. Pallas,

Many thanks for your lovely Christmas greetings. We too wish you and your husband all the best, especially good health for the upcoming New Year.

By the way, in January my nephew from Oregon will come for a second time to visit. I also expect again my sister from Colorado in the springtime 2005. She has been here already several times.

I have to thank you again for your efforts to bring my family together.

Sincerely,

Yours,

Gisela Wiltfang.

Seven years went by. We exchanged Christmas and New Year's greetings. Mrs. Wiltfang moved to Cuxhaven and Rudi and I moved to New Mexico.

The other day I called Germany and caught Mrs. Wiltfang by surprise. She was excited to hear from us. And during our conversation I asked about her sister. She told me the following:

"Yes, my sister visited us few times, but somehow I realized that she recently acted strange and I cannot figure out what is going on. She lied to me in the past about her marriages. I knew only about two, but then I learned that she was four times married. She had four children, three boys and one girl. The relationship to her daughter is estranged since approximately. ten years."

Mrs. Wiltfang asked me to call her sister, Mrs. Reid, who had changed her name back to her maiden name, Eder. Via email, Mrs. Wiltfang sent me her sister's address and telephone number.

I called her on Sept. 18, 2011, in Durango, Colorado. She remembered me and was talkative. She explained to me that due to a stroke and heavy medication she had difficulty in moving around. She couldn't even take a part-time job which would help her financially.

This seemed to explain why the communication with her sister in Germany had been interrupted.

I also asked her about the children, and Mrs. Eder confirmed that she had not spoken to her daughter from her first marriage for ten years. She didn't even know her daughter's married name or her address in New Mexico. She said her sons lived in Oregon, California and Durango.

We promised each other to stay in contact and I told her that there would be a possibility for us to visit her. She said she would like to meet us in person.

I wrote an email to Mrs. Wiltfang in Germany describing the conversation I had with Mrs. Eder. I hope that she will not be worried anymore about the silence which occurred between them.

Chapter 26
Miracle – A New Family

For many years since Rudi told me he had children from his first marriage I was eager to find them. I knew Rudi was missing them, but he never complained. Occasionally I talked to Rudi's friends in Holland about it, and they promised to help me in this search.

On Christmas Eve 2004, among many other holiday cards we received, one was from our friends Bavo and Dineke in Holland. Dineke tried to help in the search for Rudi's children who had disappeared with their mother after the divorce. I wanted to know what happened afterwards and where they were. I realized many times that Rudi had a special heart and connection for children he met. He liked to play with them no matter how old they were, healthy or even disabled, such as the son of my cousin.

The Christmas card contained the address of Rudi's daughter Danielle. Dineke had gotten it through acquaintances in Canada. According to the information, Danielle, was married and living in New Hampshire. We discussed this surprising news and tried to decide how to approach Danielle. Rudi was excited, but also afraid that his daughter might not accept his call.

In this case I dialed the number. A woman's voice answered the call. I asked:

"Do I talk to Danielle?"

"No, this is Joyce," was the answer.

"My name is Irma Pallas and I am calling from Cincinnati," I continued.

Then I passed the phone to Rudi. Joyce was his ex-wife. The first part of their conversation was stumbled in English, German or Dutch, but continued in English in a friendly matter. Danielle was not home, but her mother promised that she would call upon her arrival. Rudi left our phone number. Joyce also mentioned that their son Arvid lived in Florida and had joined the Air Force.

Later in the afternoon Danielle called while Rudi walked the dog. We talked briefly until Rudi came home. He continued the conversation. She seemed to be surprised, in shock and not very talkative, which she confirmed the next day in her email.

"I was shocked that you exist" was her explanation for not being so open. "I do not have children. I just went through a divorce," she continued. She also promised to contact her brother Arvid.

On Sunday, December 26, 2005, we hosted friends from Wisconsin. In the afternoon Arvid called. The first impression was pleasant. The conversation very open and longer compared to the one with Danielle. He gave Rudi the rundown about his life, education, marriage and job. From this moment on, email correspondence started which will follow in a diary style.

December 27, 2004 from Irma to Danielle
Hello Danielle,

Allow me to send you a brief message. Your dad had to leave for Cleveland, but he will send you an email tomorrow. He was very excited to hear from your brother Arvid. Yes, I think there is a lot to catch up on. Believe me it was the nicest Christmas present for him.

Certainly, it is a shock and surprise for you, but we tried everything since 1988 but did not know where to start. Recently I brought a family together after 30 years, but at least I knew where to search for (location, married name and immigration entry port). We did not know anything about you.

Rumors told us to search either in Canada, Mexico, USA and even Indonesia. To make it short, stay in touch.

Happy New Year. Fondly, Irma Pallas

December 27, 2004 from Irma to Arvid
Hello Arvid,
Allow me to drop a note since your dad had to leave for Cleveland. He will be in touch with you from there. It was really nice to hear from you and for your dad it was very emotional. He never talked much but always kept it inside.

I was searching for you kids without telling him much. It was a very hard and a difficult time when he lost you. Then his estranged mother also gave him additional problems which are behind him now. He loves his job; customers respect him and his knowledge is very satisfying. I hope very much that the relationship between you both will grow and remain as sincere as possible. I also look forward to meet you and your wife.

Stay in touch. Sincerely, Irma Pallas

January 3, 20005 from Arvid
Hi Dad,
I'm excited about your visit and am happy that it will be earlier than March. Paulla and I are looking forward to visiting with both of you. We will be happy to pick you up at the airport, but may need a flight number or connecting city. There are several flights from Delta that arrive here in Pensacola and most flights connect through Atlanta, Charlotte, or Memphis before arriving here. We could also check on-line to see if there were any flight delays. We have plenty of room here at the house and hope you planned to stay with us. If there is

anything we can do to help with your visit or anything you may need while you are here please ask.

I know we'll get better acquainted on your visit, but I hope I could ask a few questions. Do you have any hobbies or interests you enjoy? When is your birthday? I was also curious if you had any photos of us when we were in Holland? I'm sure I'll have a lot more questions when you visit so that's probably enough for now. I hope your trip to Cleveland went well and that the snow conditions up in Cincinnati are getting better. We look forward to seeing you soon.

Sincerely,
Your son, Arvid

January 5, 2005 from Arvid
Hello,
Thank you so much for your email. I understand there were some problems with my email address, but I am glad to see it was straightened out. I was happy to hear you enjoyed Christmas and I hope you and Irma have a wonderful New Year.

It was definitely a surprise to hear from you after all these years, but is was also a great Christmas gift for me. I was thrilled to finally speak with you at Christmas and regret that it did not happen sooner. I had asked about you when I was much younger, but did not get very much information and some of the information I did get was incorrect. However, all that is in the past and Paulla and I look forward to meeting you and your wife.

I think the end of February or beginning of March should be a great time and the weather here would be very nice as well. I will be in Washington D.C. for work from February 9th through the 13th, but will be home the rest of the month. Please let me know when you've made your flight arrangements.

Irma Pallas

Our address is: Arvid & Paulla Opry, 7224 Tannehill Dr. Pensacola, FL 32526 Phone – (850) 944-7150.

We are very interested in learning more about you both and are looking forward to speaking with you in person. I've included two photos of when Paulla and I were in Arizona this spring and a Christmas photo with our dog Maddy. Please let me know if you can open them or I will send them again. I would very much like to have a picture of you both and I plan to stay in touch. Please e-mail, call, or write anytime.

Sincerely,
Your son, Arvid

January 5, 2005 from Rudi to Arvid
Hi, Arvid and Paulla,

Thanks for the nice picture. In return I will also attach some pictures. I have made reservations for Irma and I on a flight to Pensacola for the weekend February 19-20. Arriving Saturday 2-19-05 at 11.53 a.m. with Delta/Comair at Pensacola, the return flight is on Sunday 2-20-05 at 6.45 p.m. We hope it is o.k. with you. We are very excited to meet you and get acquainted. It will work out with our dog since he is due with his shots and teeth cleaning. The Vet has the possibilities for boarding as well.

In the meantime we can continue with our e-mail correspondence. Again, I am glad to be in touch with you.

Regards,
Your dad, Rudi

January 5, 2005 From Rudi to Arvid
Hi Arvid and Paulla,

Yes, we are glad to stay with you. I booked a direct flight from Cincinnati to Pensacola on Saturday Feb. 9th, Delta 5412 arriving at 11.53 a.m. We will call you when we leave Cincinnati (approx. 10.00 a.m.)

Ordinary Woman

My hobbies and interests are photography, history and traveling. Lately we are not traveling that much, Irma is too occupied with her job as a spare parts manager.

My birthday is on April 12th and Irma's is on July 31st, both born in 1941. I have only a few photos with you and Danielle from the time in Holland.

I am again back in Cleveland; hopefully this job will be finished by the end of January/first week in February.

The weather here is again snow mixed with ice. When I left Cincinnati all the snow was gone, at least we had a nice white Christmas.

This is for today, give Paulla a hug.

Your Dad, Rudi

January 9, 2005 from Rudi to Arvid
Dear Arvid,

I received an e-mail today from Danielle. As I can see, you talked to each other and she anticipates going to Pensacola as well. Attached please find my response to her. It may also answer some of your questions. Stay in touch and kind regards,

Your Dad, Rudi

January 9, 2005 from Rudi to Danielle
Dear Danielle,

Thank you very much for your e-mail dated 8th. I am very pleased to hear that you plan to meet us at Arvid's home in Pensacola. It would be a good opportunity to talk to both of you at the same time and answer your questions. But in case you can't make it, there will be another time pretty soon.

In regard to your last question: No I don't have any other children.

My hobbies are photography, travel and history. We both like to read, and enjoy good music.

I still work for the same German company in the service department as I worked when I lived in the Netherlands. After the divorce I was assigned to install and service our machines almost in all Europe and around the world.

In 1980 I was dispatched for 1 year to the US to service customers out of the Milwaukee office. From 1985 until 1991 Chicago was my base. I remarried in 1987 in Chicago. My wife is German as well and works as a spare parts manager in the same company. In the summer of 1991 we went back to Germany for 5 years for our company in order to establish a service center in south Germany.

In 1997 we moved back to Milwaukee and in 2001 the company relocated us to Cincinnati. Our company is making Tool Machines, the customers are Caterpillar, GM, Ford and Daimler Chrysler. Lately we are strongly engaged in the aircraft business (Boeing and Lockheed etc).

At the moment I am in Cleveland, overhauling a big machine. Hopefully this job will be finished end of January/beginning of February.

Arvid has sent me a picture of him and Paulla; do you have a picture of yourself available for me? The only photo I have from you is when you were approx. 4 years old and Arvid 2 years.

I hope this answers some of your questions.

Again I would be pleased to see you as well on February 9th at Arvid's home. Please stay in touch. Until then best regards,

Your Dad, Rudi

January 10, 2005 from Arvid
Hi Dad,
Yes, I spoke to Danielle this weekend and told her how we've emailed and made plans for the end of February. I forwarded her your email with the flight itinerary and days you'll be visiting. I hope it was OK. She told me that she had planned on being in South Carolina around the same time and

wanted to come for your visit. I thought it would be OK and I asked that she should tell you.

She said that she hadn't sent you any other emails so I told her to email you with her plans. I haven't heard back from her, but I think she'll be here a few days before you arrive.

Thank you for providing information about yourself in the emails. They answer some questions and I feel I'm getting to know you a little better. I'm sure Danielle and I will still have questions, but I look forward to seeing you and just spending time together. I was thinking yesterday about how long it's been and can't believe it. It is really a miracle.

I thought I would let you know some information about myself. After leaving the Netherlands, we lived in Texas till 1988. We then moved to Arizona where I stayed until I graduated from Arizona State University. I received a degree in Mathematics and became a commissioned officer in the U.S. Air Force. I married Paulla in 1996 and went to flight school in Florida. I have been stationed in San Antonio, Texas, Little Rock, Arkansas, and Tucson, Arizona. I finished my Masters Degree in Management in 2002 and am currently an instructor back in Florida at flight school. Some of my interests include woodworking, camping, and spending time outdoors.

Take care and give my best to Irma
Your son, Arvid

January 14, 2005 from Danielle
I don't have any photos of myself that I can email to you. I will be able to see you in February in Pensacola. I'll coordinate my arrival with Arvid, but I'll come before you do on Saturday. If I find some photos of me, I'll bring them with me to give to you.
Danielle

January 16, 2005 from Arvid

It was great to hear from you again and I always look forward (and enjoy) getting email from you. I'm glad that you recognized that I'm eager to meet you and spend time getting to know you and Irma. Although I have had a very fortunate life, I would very much like to make up for lost time. It is strange to hear about my life in Holland so long ago. I guess I haven't thought about it very often until recently. We did have a strong European influence in our youth growing up with our grandparents. However, Mom, Danielle and I don't speak about the Netherlands or Europe very often since my grandparents passed away. I did spend a few months in Italy on a military deployment. During that time I was able to tour Venice a few times as well as ski along the border in Austria. I absolutely loved Europe and look forward to taking Paulla there some time. I have always been interested in my past, but have mostly spent time focusing on the future. Going to school, getting married, working and so forth have kept me very busy.

Paulla wanted to make sure I mention that you're very accurate about me and Danielle. I don't think we're too different, but I guess Danielle has always been more cautious and reserved. Sometimes I wish she could be a little friendlier or open even with Paulla. She might not make friends as quickly as I do, but I have been blessed with such great friends growing up. I usually don't want to miss opportunities to meet new people and get to know them. Being in the military, Paulla and I move quite often, so there isn't a lot of time for us to make new friends so it helps to give people a chance. I agree with you about being open minded and positive and I think Danielle will be too. It might take a little more time. I think she will make the plane reservations and should be able to join us in February.

As far as Maddy...she is a golden retriever born in August of 2003. We picked her up at 7 weeks and now is almost 17 months. I almost always had a dog growing up, but haven't had one since I went away to college. I had always been anxious to get a dog, but Paulla never had any pets. It took a little time to convince her, especially since being in the military I travel and am away from home often. I didn't want Paulla taking care of the dog while I was away. I finally convinced her to look. Although Paulla may have wanted a smaller dog, we decided to look at some different breeds. It's funny, but we only went to one breeder and saw Maddy.

After seeing her, we didn't need to look any further. She was perfect and has become a member of the family (and quite spoiled) I've included a favorite photo of her as a puppy at about 8 pounds and one while we were camping early last year. She's almost fully grown now and a trim 70 pounds. What a different a year makes! We are definitely dog people as well.

Regards,
Your son, Arvid

As of that date emails were exchanged almost on daily basis. We visited Arvid and Paulla in Florida on February 29, 2005. Danielle joined the meeting.

We arrived by plane and they were delayed due to traffic reasons. Arvid and Paulla embraced us while Danielle seemed to be a little reserved.

After a short lunch we continued to their home. Father and the kids sat down in one corner of the room und started to talk, ask questions and give some explanation. We learned a lot about their past. Yes, it was confirmed that grandmother was the one who kept the discipline in the family, intrigued between the siblings and her own daughter—mother of the kids. Once in a while I interrupted with a question or remark, but otherwise I stayed with Paulla to the side.

The children's mother, Joyce, never grew up or stood up to her own mother. She gave up playing the piano because she was not good enough, according to her mother. All the negative remarks resulted later in poor health such as panic attacks, depression, diabetes, and stomach problems. Joyce also mentioned to her children that due to the strong influence of her own mother she divorced Rudi and was not able to start a new relationship. She needed frequent treatments.

Danielle had to take her mother into her house in order to care and help her to master her life. According to Danielle's statement, her mother was in a childhood state of mind, forgetting things, and spending money for unnecessary items. There was no communication in the house, and that gave Danielle the feeling of being alone.

Danielle continued about her life was. She divorced after ten years of marriage, and had quit her job as software engineer in order to save her marriage, which she regretted badly. It was hard and difficult to find another job, and her savings were not enough to continue.

There was also anger and bitterness towards her brother about the past. He had parted from the family and did not help in caring for the ailing grandparents.

Paulla, Arvid's wife, addressed several questions to Danielle, but made also a statement which was based on knowledge from her husband. A dialogue continued which resulted in clarification of many unspoken details. As a listener, I was glad to see that tension start to diminish.

Arvid and Danielle managed to finish their education in spite of the hard and poor life conditions. Both took jobs in order to pay for their education. Arvid finished his education in Arizona and achieved two university degrees. Then he went to the Air Force, where he passed flight training, continued in the navigation field and advanced from captain to a major. Later on followed schooling in Alabama, and today he is working at the Pentagon.

The following day, Sunday, we three women were sitting together and still discussing the unspoken childhood problems. Danielle clarified some statements made by her brother, which explained also the bitterness she feels regarding the past.

I had the impression that our visit not only brought father and children together, but also helped to improve the relationship between the siblings.

We parted Sunday evening. Arvid came one more time to the terminal and thanked me for finding the children. We invited them all to our house for the Memorial Day weekend in 2005.

It was the most beautiful and sincere weekend. Both arrived on Saturday from different directions. We went home first to settle in. In the afternoon we invited them for dinner at the Hofbraeuhaus at the other side of the Ohio River in Newport, Kentucky. It was a fun afternoon; good food and music made them all feel at ease.

The evening we spent at home talking and exchanging experiences. We showed photo albums from our trips to Hawaii, Argentina, South Africa etc. Paulla had never left the States. Arvid had been in Greece due to his deployment by the Air Force, but had never visited Holland or Germany. Therefore, we suggested taking them to Europe in 2006 for their tenth anniversary.

We want to show them Holland where they were born and Germany. Paulla's question came:

"Are we going to Paris too?" Rudi and I looked at each other and we both said, "Why not?" It had been a long time since we had been there and we would enjoy it as well.

On Sunday we had plans for a boat ride on the Ohio River with brunch. The weather was spectacular. We took a lot of pictures, enjoyed the brunch and the entertainment.

In the afternoon we showed them our company office and the old town of Loveland.

With our dog Riley we had a nice walk back home. Everybody could relax while I prepared a German dish for supper.

The atmosphere was very relaxed and everybody went satisfied to bed.

On Monday, Memorial Day, we did a little shopping, and in the late afternoon I arranged a little cocktail party. Three couples from our neighborhood were invited, and a single lady as well. Everybody, of course, was eager to meet the children. A lot of laughter came up since common acquaintances were discovered.

Summarizing this weekend I can say it was positive by all means. They took a lot of impressions home and learned about us and our lifestyle. Both parties left on Tuesday; Danielle in the morning, and Arvid and Paulla in the evening.

We visited Danielle in the fall and had another family gathering over Christmas in Tucson, Arizona. Arvid had been transferred and he needed to establish a new home, which was being built at that time. We all were excited and decided to continue our still fresh relationship.

Chapter 27
The First Anniversary

It was Christmas time 2005 and we prepared a trip to Arizona. Exactly a year before we had gotten the good news telling us the whereabouts of Rudi's children.

The year was full of excitements. We met the children in Florida, the kids came to Cincinnati over the Memorial Day weekend, and in October we visited daughter Danielle in New Hampshire. Son Arvid had been transferred from Florida to Tucson, Arizona. Now it was time to get ready and hit the road.

The drive from Cincinnati to Tucson took about three days by car with stops in Arkansas, Texas and New Mexico. The weather couldn't have been better. The stops at the visitor centers contributed to road information, weather conditions and accommodations. It was important to us to find hotels with a swimming pool for relaxation after a long ride.

On Christmas Eve, in the late morning, we reached our destination, Tucson. Arvid greeted us on the street. The house he and Paulla bought was located in a new subdivision. They were lucky that with all the delays they had been able to move in two days before Christmas Eve. Except for a few unpacked boxes in the garage, everything was in place and arranged very tastefully.

Before we started our trip I told Paulla and Arvid:

"As long we have a bed to sleep on it, we do not care if everything is organized."

Everything was better than we expected. Paulla did a good job and chose matching colors of paint, wall decoration, bathroom arrangements, and last but not least, proved to be a good hostess.

"I will help you to set up the Christmas tree," I told her. And yes indeed she agreed and accepted my and Rudi's help. We had fun, and in no time the tree was up and fully decorated.

For dinner Paulla prepared a wonderful dish and we sat and talked for a while and retired early. Everybody was exhausted; Rudi and I after the long drive, and Arvid and Paulla after rushing to move in.

On Christmas morning, we all got up at seven in the morning and sat down in our pajamas with cups of coffee. Christmas presents were distributed. We had a lot of fun. Everybody was so spontaneous.

After breakfast we decided to take a trip for sightseeing and visit a mall known for handcrafting and boutiques. In one of those I bought a cowboy hat for which I have always been complimented.

In the afternoon, Paulla expected guests for Christmas dinner. She prepared a delicious ham and the guests contributed with their special dishes. It was a pleasant and fun atmosphere that included interesting conversations. Among the guests was one retired couple from the Air Force and Paulla's ladyfriend Jane.

Next morning, Arvid showed us the Air Force base and their trailer, which was parked in the base's parking lot next to many others of different sizes. Retired Air Force members come and go with their RVs.

After that we continued to the Santa Catalina National Park and took a little tram up the mountains and admired the wonderful landscape. People were hiking, but after a while they went with the tram uphill and then down to the station. We took several pictures next to the cactus to show how huge they are.

Paulla's parents came to visit and met us for the first time. I connected with Mimi, Paulla's mom, immediately. We had a glass of champagne and got acquainted. Unfortunately, the telephone rang and the message came that their house had been broken into and burglarized. Bill, Paulla's dad, wanted to go home immediately. It was a trip of four hours to Snowflake, Arizona, where they lived. We understood the situation and we promised to find another chance to visit and catch up.

Next day was time to part since we wanted to be back home before New Year's. On the way we planned to visit the oil field museum while passing through Texas. Here we learned a lot on how the oil was pumped and sent to refineries for processing.

The weather was perfect, nice and warm. We made some stops for refreshments and took pictures. It took us forever to get to the hotel in Fort Worth due to traffic jams.

Then we continued to Arkansas with the goal to stay overnight in Hot Springs. On the way we visited the birthplace of President Bill Clinton in Hope.

The schedule was tight and did not give us enough time to spend in Hot Springs. Early the next day we left Hot Springs, and passed Memphis, and Louisville. We arrived very late home in Loveland, Ohio.

It was a long and exhausting trip, but we enjoyed each minute of it.

In the meantime, Arvid was deployed once on the rush basis to Columbia, South America, and three times to Kuwait. It was a tough time for Paulla, but also for us since we were worried about him. We were glad to have him back in the States.

Arvid was very ambitious, and therefore, he enrolled into the Military School in Montgomery, Alabama. This was the last educational step prior to be accepted to the Pentagon. He moved to Washington, D.C., in the fall of 2010. In December 2010, Arvid and Paulla visited us for Christmas, and we were excited to participate in his promotion ceremony to lieutenant colonel on August 31, 2011.

Chapter 28
European Vacation with the Children in 2006

It started with a promise to the children during their Memorial Day visit in Cincinnati in 2005. We talked about future plans and how to introduce them to their European roots. Since such planning needed time, we tentatively set a timeframe for late spring in 2006. This was also supposed to be a gift for the tenth wedding anniversary of Arvid and Paulla, as well as a late present for Rudi's sixty-fifth birthday. Everybody agreed, including Danielle, who was eager to join us.

Paulla had never been overseas. She had visited neighboring countries Canada and Mexico, but no others. We could see her excitement. When Rudi suggested a route through Germany and Netherlands, Paulla's question popped out:

"Are we going to Paris as well?"

Rudi and I looked at each other and thought it was a good idea. I had been three times to Paris, but many years before. Each time that city, with its flair and atmosphere, greeted me in a positive way. We promised Paulla to include Paris into our schedule.

The trip was as important to me as it was for Rudi. It gave us the opportunity to expand and deepen our relationship with the children. I never had children of my own due to many different circumstances (health, being in different locations and unhappy relationships). In the beginning it was difficult to develop motherly feelings, therefore, I decided to be a friend and a link between Rudi and his children. I think I was successful and I enjoy the connection to each of the children.

Rudi started to investigate and plan this trip, which took him two months. We also purchased two DVDs covering European countries, especially Germany, Netherlands, and, of course, Paris. These DVDs and an overview of the travel plans were submitted to the children in order for them to schedule their vacation time and get prepared and to get acquainted with the countries we wanted to visit. The only expenses they had to cover were the flight tickets to and from Frankfurt, Germany. We all were supposed to meet at this destination. All other expenses such as car rentals, hotel accommodations and meals we planned to cover.

Finally, the twenty-fifth of April, 2006, was the departure date. Rudi and I left one day earlier, rented a van and picked up the children in the morning of April twenty-six. Danielle arrived first at 5.20 a.m., while Arvid and Paulla's plane touched down at seven in the morning.

We loaded the luggage to the van and drove to our friend Doris, in Gelnhausen, forty minutes away from the Frankfurt airport. Doris prepared a German breakfast which included cold cuts, boiled eggs and German bread.

We all were a little tired, having had little sleep due to the long flight and time change. Still, we decided to take a historical walk through the town of Gelnhausen.

The weather was rainy and chilly, but it did not matter to us; it was good to move a little and exercise our legs. We still had some driving hours ahead. Doris was very pleased to host our family and served a small lunch before we wrapped up and continued on our journey.

The next stop was to be in Muenster, Westphalia, where we met Rudi's cousin, Uschi, who was expecting us and had made hotel reservations. Uschi was an orthopedic surgeon. I had met her only once before in Augsburg; it was her last practice time before her graduation into the orthopedic faculty.

Uschi had been a physical therapist for many years. However, her ambition led her to higher goals and the study of medicine at the age of thirty-eight. She was born in Berlin, and, therefore, inherited the Berlin temper (which was disliked in other parts of Germany). She liked to criticize and argue, even on job sites. A very independent, sporty and intelligent person, she gave a more masculine impression. She never married, traveled around the world with friends, and her favored sport was diving, which almost took her life. She was even proud of telling us about dangerous risks she liked to take. In addition, I disliked her loud voice.

Uschi had just started a job at the children's hospital in Muenster. Here again, after a short time, we had to listen to her complaints about the chief surgeon who corrected and tried to teach her certain ways of how to operate. As we expected, she did not last long there. The next message from her came from Berlin. Since this was her home city, and she always wanted to return there, she was lucky to accept an offer and later on work independently.

Beside the point, we still enjoyed being with her. She showed and explained a few things about this city of Muenster before we retired to a very traditional restaurant for dinner. It was the season of white asparagus, which is not so well known in the States. We all chose an asparagus dish with different side orders such as ham, schnitzel or just Hollandaise sauce. The atmosphere was pleasant with a lot of laughter.

Muenster is a city with plenty of history as well as shopping opportunities and green spaces for cycling, inline skating or golfing. There is a unique supply of activities to enjoy art and culture alongside other pleasures. We walked through the Old Town, which is alive with architectural culture from nine centuries. The historic center is a place where people from all walks of life and different cultural backgrounds meet and get to know each other.

On Friday, April 28, we had planned to arrive in Meerbusch, close to Duesseldorf, which was our next station. My sister Karin and husband wanted to meet us. Unfortunately, we had some car problems which we had to solve in Muenster. This delayed our arrival about two hours. Of course, Karin was upset and could not understand that something like that could happen, but unexpected things can occur.

For three years my mother had been in a nursing home in Meerbusch and I wanted to be there with her, therefore, we decided that Rudi and the children would go by train to Koeln (Cologne) on Saturday while I would stay with my mother. Her health was very poor. She was very weak and hardly talked or responded in speech. This was a very sad visit. But I still think that she recognized me, especially when I addressed a few Polish words to her, which she understood and knew they came from me.

When we arrived in Meerbusch I was surprised by a friend whom I knew from Poland and who was waiting for me at the hotel. Due to the delay of our arrival we had only a few minutes to talk and I promised that we would meet on Saturday evening in Duesseldorf. He was Lech (Leszek). We had known each other over thirty years and we had not seen each other for twenty-four years. I met him in Warsaw in 1972 while attending a cabaret performance. He was a dancer as well as pianist in the show. I would describe him as a very funny, intelligent, and an open-minded person.

We grew close to each other and I also was privileged to meet his whole family which resided in Chestochowa, a city known for pilgrimages by Catholics who were praying to the Black Madonna located in the church on the hill.

On Saturday, while I stayed with mom, Rudi and the children left by train to Cologne where a friend of ours was waiting to show them the city. They just loved it. Cologne is a beautiful and diverse city, surrounded by an equally attractive and varied countryside. Cologne stands on ground that is steeped in history. The children visited the Cologne Dom (cathedral) and could not get enough of it. They enjoyed lunch and many other attractions.

In the evening we drove to Dusseldorf, as we had promised my fried Lech to see him. I liked Lech from the first moment I met him because of his personality, humor and experience as a dancer, musician and singer. Our friendship over the years and distances never died, and it seemed like we had parted just yesterday. At the Hotel Steigenberger, Lech was playing the piano at the bar. It is one the most famous hotels in Dusseldorf. Lech knew that we would arrive late, therefore, he made sure that there was a reserved parking space for us. We had a drink and spent two hours together. Lech spoke fluent German and English and we all could participate in the conversation. When we parted, we promised each other to stay in touch and meet again.

On Sunday, April 30, we continued our trip to Odijk in Holland where our friends Bavo and Dieneke were expecting us. On the way we stopped in Roemond at a big outlet mall and Paulla was able to find comfortable walking shoes. In the meantime, Danielle and Arvid walked through the town where they were born. We also showed them the homes that they lived in as children. This was very emotional for Danielle, the older of the children, who remembered sadder, rather than happier times.

The welcome by our friends in Odijk was outstanding. Dineke prepared an open bar with snacks. Remco, Dineke's son, his lovely girlfriend Melina and their daughter were there, as were Sietske (Dineke's daughter) with her husband Ted. For me it was emotional to see them. Bavo welcomed us with a champagne toast for our family reunion. But he did not only point out our family, we talked about the time he remembered when Rudi and his family were still in the Netherlands.

Bavo and Dineke hosted us for three days in the most wonderful way. They showed us around and answered all our questions. It was a new experience to see the new recovered land (New Land), Keukenhof, the tulip paradise, and also Amsterdam. Beside the rainy day, everybody enjoyed it. Last but not least, we all admired our friend's new sailboat as well.

On the last evening, Sietske, the daughter, and her husband Ted joined us for dinner. Sietske announced that she was pregnant with her second child, another excitement. Before they left, we took family pictures and I did not miss keeping my video camera going. Soon the nice time in Holland came to an end.

From Holland we continued to the Moselle Valley, where the river curves between two hiking paradises, Eifel and Hunsrueck. We decided to stay in one of the hotels in Cochem, Waldhotel Winningen, which was located away from the main traffic area. Behind the hotel there was a creek from where we got rainbow trout for dinner. The owner, who was also a cook, prepared for each of us a different trout dish, and it was delicious. There was not enough time to visit the surroundings and remains of the old town wall.

Prior to our arrival in Cochem we had the chance to visit Burg Elz (castle) which was an unbelievable experience for everyone. We attended a tour through the castle and at the end we enjoyed a cold beer in the castle's beer garden.

The following day, Thursday, we continued towards the city of Kaiserslautern. There we anticipated to meet Arvid's friend, Eric, who was stationed at the Air Force base. Rudi made a reservation at the Novotel Hotel. Since we arrived in the afternoon, Arvid and Eric left for the base. They had not seen each other for a while and had a lot to talk about. We girls and Rudi decided to go shopping. The stores in Germany closed at 6.30 p.m., therefore, we had to rush. We took a cab to the shopping area. It was fun and everybody bought a few items. Danielle bought a skirt and a twin set, Paulla bought

Ordinary Woman

Capri pants and I got a skirt and some tops. Rudi found a nice t-shirt as well. Finally, the closing time was announced and we rushed home in order to meet the boys at the hotel bar.

In the evening Eric joined us for dinner in the hotel restaurant. According to the menu, the food seemed to be excellent, and it was indeed. Eric learned how to handle a fish dish and we all laughed a lot and had a good time.

Unfortunately, we did not have time to learn more about the city of Kaiserslauter, which is located in southwest Germany in the Bundesland (state) of Rheinland-Pfalz. Kaiserslautern is home to 99,469 people. In the city and its surrounding district lived an additional 50,000 NATO military personnel members (mainly Americans). This city had a lot of history to tell, but today, Kaiserslautern is a modern center of information and communications technology, a well-known university, a technical college and many international research institutes.

On Friday morning, May fifth, we had to rush to the train. The hotel personnel helped us to store our luggage away, and everybody just took a carry-on bag. Our car remained at the hotel parking lot and we anticipated staying one more night upon returning from Paris.

We took a train to Paris. Our friend Doris purchased round-trip tickets for us and reserved a compartment as well. The travel duration was about four hours. The main train station in Paris was huge and crowded with all kinds of people of different nationalities. The next task was to find the Metro station and get acquainted with the purchase of tickets and learn about the different directions—line numbers. We found the correct line number and station where to disembark. It was a short walk to the hotel, which was located on a narrow side street. The outside façade showed its age, but was very well kept. Inside it was cozy, remodeled, and equipped with an elevator to the sixth floor. The rooms were tastefully decorated and were small but comfortable. The breakfast was served in the basement, reminding us of catacombs. Service was excellent and people were very polite. We also were able to check our emails since the Internet was available in this hotel.

That same day we went to lunch at a nearby restaurant, and after that we walked to the Eiffel Tower. It is the symbol for this city, which was erected on the occasion of the World Fair in 1889.

We were told that although 1,050 feet high, the Eiffel Tower is an extremely light structure. It has three floors: the first at hundred eighty-seven feet, the second at three hundred seventy-seven feet and the third at eight hundred ninety-nine feet. On each floor there were bars and restaurants. We did not go up. It was late, and too many people were in line. Our day ended with a dinner in a Brasserie. We all slept well that night. It was indeed a long day.

Saturday, May 6, we decided to visit the Notre Dame Cathedral. It is a Gothic style cathedral dating as early as 1200. The interior is four hundred twenty-six feet long, one hundred sixty-four feet wide, and one hundred fifteen feet high. It can accommodate about nine thousand people. It is important to point out the South Rose Window as a work of the thirteenth century. The colors and precise placing of the glass gave the impression that an intensely bright star was bursting. It was amazing to see something so beautiful.

From there we decided to see the Arch of Triumph which was located at the end of the Champs-Elysees. It was a powerful and imposing arch, one hundred sixty-four feet high and a hundred forty-seven feet wide. The children went up the stairs and had a wonderful view of Paris.

I remained on the street level. A Japanese group of people with cameras hanging over their chests pushed their way through and caused me to fall against an iron guarding, which hurt my head badly. My glasses fell off. An American tourist who witnessed it came to help me up and was worried. He stayed close to me and asked several times if I was okay. I was okay, but had a bad bump like a horn, blue and greenish colored. I felt a little dizzy but did not want to worry Rudi and the children.

We concluded the day with a Seine River boat tour, which was another attraction passing under the oldest bridge Pont Neuf completed in 1606. The tour went around Cathedral Island and along the river banks. Museums and important buildings were pointed out by the tourist guide. A sudden rain shower made us cuddle together under the boat's roof, but as soon as we returned to the boat station the rain stopped and we walked satisfied towards the hotel, but did not miss stopping at a store to buy water and fruits. Before we retired to our rooms we made plans for the next day and decided to go early to the Louvre.

It was a day with free admittance and we wanted to avoid the crowds, but when we arrived we had to join the super long line which surprisingly moved quickly.

The Louvre dated back to the thirteenth century and was built in sections. It still shows various phases of constructions. It was more or less finished under Napoleon. Inside we had to get acquainted with the structure of the wings and exhibitions. The first thing we saw, as did every other visitor, was Leonardo da Vinci's Mona Lisa. This painting was guarded tremendously by museum personnel. It was behind a heavy glass frame and had an alarm installation. It was not as big as we had imagined.. The crowd moved slowly around and was very disciplined. We then decided to part because everyone wanted to see particular paintings. We met for lunch and exchanged our opinions. It was too much and to exhausting to see everything, but by the end of the day we all were happy and very much impressed with the great works of art. Rudi and I walked slowly back towards our hotel, but on the way we stopped at one of the outside cafes for a glass of wine. We enjoyed watching people promenading in front of us.

When we continued our walk, we discovered a very nice restaurant and decided to make a reservation for our last evening in Paris. The restaurant's name was Chien de Fume. Upon arrival at the hotel, everyone was refreshed and changed from tourist clothing into something more formal, and we walked to the restaurant. We decided that everyone would have a different dish in order to get acquainted with the French cuisine. Service was excellent, there were no language barriers, and in general we could say that people were very friendly. It was a successful evening which pleasantly closed the Paris chapter.

On Monday, May eighth, we still had some time to kill before we had to catch our train. Therefore, I suggested we visit the famous church Sacre Coeure, which was majestically located on the hill of Montmartre overlooking the city of Paris. We left our luggage at the hotel, took the Metro and visited the church, that was erected in 1876. To reach it, we could either take the steps or a rail cabin. The children were amazed to see the interior, because of its decorations of paintings and mosaics. They also could not resist climbing up to the upper dome where they had the opportunity to walk around.

It was now time to return to the hotel, get the luggage and approach the train station back to Kaiserslautern where we arrived at 9.15 p.m. We took a cab to the hotel and met Eric one more time. He arrived with six bottles of German wine for the children to take with them. Still, we settled for a short and late dinner, but retired soon because we all were tired and exhausted.

On Tuesday, May ninth, our journey continued towards Ruedesheim along the river Rhein. We checked into one of the hotels. The hostess informed us that one more boat tour was leaving soon, and this we did not want to miss. It was such a relaxing and spectacular tour. We passed many of the old castles, either as ruins or still intact. The hilly landscape was inviting. When we returned, we went to the famous Drossel Gasse, a very narrow alley with restaurants, shops and bou-

Ordinary Woman

tiques. Rudi and I knew the restaurant of the Schlosshotel Ruedesheim with a particular atmosphere.

We had dinner and enjoyed the live music, and the children sang along with songs that were played for tourists. When walking out of the beer garden, Arvid and Paulla could not resist having a dance on the street. It gave us a good feeling that everything had turned out perfect. The nicest complement by Paulla was: "I liked Paris, but Germany and the food was the best."

On Wednesday, May tenth, we left Ruedesheim early in the morning and we brought the children to the Frankfurt airport. Arvid, Paulla and Danielle left almost at the same time. I made sure that they found the correct airline counters to check in and said a quick goodbye so as to not get emotional.

After that Rudi and I visited my cousin Ruth for lunch in Offenbach. More family members joined us. It was good to see Christian, the son of my late cousin Josel. I had not seen Christian for twenty years. Memories were refreshed and we decided to meet again a year later when we returned to Germany for another visit.

The last night we spent with Doris, who was eager to hear how everything had gone. She is a lovely and dear friend to us who was never too tired to do us favors, whether sending flowers to family member on their birthdays or holidays or arrange, as we needed, train tickets. She was reimbursed for the expenses she had for all the requested arrangements. Frequently we talk to her on the phone and she is pleased to hear about us and tour children.

We left on Thursday, May eleventh, in the morning. We still had to return the rented car, and with a shuttle bus we got to the airport. The flight home with Delta was pleasant. The weather was to our advantage.

Summarizing this trip I have to complement Rudi, who arranged it, because everything worked out just perfect. The video taken and photos will always remind us of how wonderful this journey was.

Today we are planning another trip with Arvid and Paulla, which tentatively will be in April 2012. This trip will cover the south part of Germany.

Chapter 29
The Wedding and Baby Alison

Almost two years had passed since we were united with Rudi's children after twenty-eight years, and the relationship could not have been better. In the meantime, Arvid, Rudi's son, was three times deployed to Kuwait. He had also had been promoted twice, first to a major and then to lieutenant colonel in the Air Force. He now works at the Pentagon.

After three years of unemployment, Danielle found a steady job as a software engineer and her life adjusted and she had a better outlook for the future.

In October 2006, Danielle called us in a happy mood. She told us that she was dating again. We learned later that she registered at e-harmony, a dating service, and had met several fellows, but only one found her approval. In November 2006, she announced that she was pregnant. Danielle said, "You are going to be grandparents." Further, she wanted us to meet her partner, Tom McIntire. We were happy for her and, at the beginning of December, Danielle and Tom visited us in Loveland, Ohio. Rudi had met him before while he was on assignment in Maine and had visited Danielle on the weekend.

Tom's family originated from Maine, but he worked in New Hampshire as a software engineer. We welcomed both to spend a weekend with us. For their visit we arranged tickets to the music hall and took them out for dinner in order to spend some time and get acquainted. Tom was not very talkative. We learned that he was an outdoors person, and had never really travelled outside of Maine or New Hampshire. The only sibling he had was Mike, who was married to a nice lady, Amanda.

Visually, Tom was a tall man, on the very heavy side, very obese, with a flat behind, but also a big belly. His jeans seemed to slide since there was no hold, and when he was bending, he was mooning everybody. We expressed concern about his health, but he insisted that he had a good health record. The McIntire family can be described nice and homey people. Tom's mom, Barbara, was five feet tall, but very much in control, while Tom's father Bill was close to six feet tall and on the heavy side as well, including the flat behind. Only Mike, Tom's brother, showed a healthy and normal body shape.

Still we realized that both, Danielle and Tom, were very much in love, and that was the most important thing.

The visit in our home went well. Before they left, we suggested to Danielle that she was welcome to spend Christmas with us. She accepted it. Since the young couple had set already the wedding date, I wanted to give her the wedding dress. This was the opportunity to go shopping.

She came, and after a long time, this was her first festive Christmas celebration. She admitted that she did not remember to have such a nice holiday. Her mother, Joyce, never cared for the Christmas atmosphere even though her own parents in Holland made sure to have a Christmas tree and some decorations, including a special dinner, and, of course, presents. Therefore, I told Rudi that this Christmas should be outstanding. I decorated the house inside and outside, a Christmas tree was decorated and found its special place. We realized that Danielle liked this cozy atmosphere and our traditional dinner consisting of salad, two kinds of fish, boiled potatoes, two different vegetables and dessert. Danielle also joined us in church for the Christmas sermon.

I took Danielle shopping. At Dillard's we found a nice wedding dress. We had to consider that it was to be on the loose side because of Danielle's pregnancy. We continued our shopping spree since she needed some other outfits for the office. It was a fun visit and we were looking forward to the wedding celebration in May 2007.

Danielle had a house in New Hampshire and Tom had his house as well. They had to decide where they would live and whether either of their homes would be big enough to accommodate them with the child and Danielle's mother. Danielle cared for her mother's health condition. They decided to sell both homes and purchase a bigger house. It was easier said than done. Tom's house was run down and needed remodeling, which took some time. Danielle's house needed some repair as well. Finally, both homes were on the market, but due to economic situation, they were sold at a loss.

A house was purchased in Pepperell, Massachusetts, which was work-wise convenient. But again, it was a neglected unit. Danielle did not care as much for the house, but for the acreage it sat on because she had horses and needed a stable and space for the horses. Danielle's hobby was, and still is, horse riding. She also attended riding competitions.

This house was in bad shape and needed a lot of work, but the layout was perfect. Since Tom was very handy, he helped Danielle, first with the stable for the horses, and then slowly with painting of some rooms in the house. Tom's father, Bill, was in construction, and helped once in a while with the remodeling.

Danielle's mother, Joyce, had to be accommodated too. Therefore, the existing garage in the lower part of the house needed to be converted into an apartment. The work started fairly quickly, however, they needed a permit for occupation. This apartment was declared as a house, bar and hobby room, and the permit finally was granted.

The time for the wedding approached and arrangements for the celebration were now a priority. The date was set for the fifth of May 2007. We were glad that Arvid was home and not deployed so he could attend the wedding together with Paulla.

On May third Rudi and I arrived in Portland, Maine, and Arvid and Paulla arrived the same morning. In the afternoon, Tom's parents invited the men to a bachelor party, while I took Danielle, her mom and Paulla to dinner at a restaurant suggested by Danielle.

We all were accommodated in the hotel, The Captain Daniel Stone Inn, in Brunswick, Maine, where the wedding ceremony took place the next day. The Captain Daniel Stone Inn had elegant guest rooms and suites where "old charm meets modern convenience," according to the description.

In the evening prior to the wedding, Tom's parents invited the family and us to the rehearsal dinner. In the morning, Tom, Daniele, Arvid, Paulla, Rudi and I went to get two dozen lobsters at the harbor as requested by Tom's mom for dinner. We observed the preparation of those lobsters. They were cooked in special pots waiting on the lawn in front of the parent's home. The weather was a bit chilly, but drinks and snacks let us forget it. The atmosphere was sincere and we all enjoyed each others company. Tom's grandfather had fun showing us tricks with the lobster eating. There was plenty of food and drinks deliciously prepared. We all parted shortly before midnight in order to get enough sleep for the next day's ceremony.

In the morning after breakfast, we took a long walk while Danielle rested.

The hotel entrance hall was nicely decorated and it was planned that the couple would come down the stairs and meet the lady reverend there.

Paulla helped Danielle with the dress, hairdo and makeup. She looked gorgeous and happy. Tom met her on the balcony and both walked down slowly. I stayed on the balcony and took pictures as well as a video. The ceremony took over an hour.

Everybody lined up to congratulate the pair as well the parents. Then pictures were taken while the guests were already seated in the ballroom. A buffet was arranged and the wedding cake had a special place.

Following the dinner, a disc jockey made sure that the music invited all for a dance. Around nine p.m., everybody parted, and we still took a nice walk around the town, and ended up in a cafe for a cup of coffee before retiring for a good night's sleep.

We decided to meet for breakfast next morning (Sunday). We said good-bye to Danielle, Tom and Joyce and left together with Arvid and Paulla towards the seashore. Our flights were in the afternoon, therefore we had enough time to visit a light house and had a nice lunch nearby. It was a small, but well known restaurant that served fish, shrimp and lobster dishes. We were seated outside but had to watch seagulls because they were attacking and stealing our food.

Finally it was time to approach the airport and catch our flights.

Danielle was eight months pregnant and was busy with preparations for the birth as well as doctor's visits. The hot weather gave her a hard time, but finally, on June 24, 2007, little Alison was born. It was a very happy moment for everyone, especially for the grandparents because it was the first grandchild.

Rudi and I visited them in late fall. It was a happy moment for Rudi to hold his first granddaughter in his arms. Alison was a friendly child, very alert and always smiling. We saw the house for the first time and realized that there was still a lot to do. In spite of the fact that both Tom and Danielle were working full time, we had the impression that remodeling and organizing was not their priority. Alison was placed in day care and Danielle picked her up after work. As Danielle described it, she was very happy and satisfied how the child was being cared for.

For Easter 2008, Danielle, Tom and Alison visited us in Cincinnati. We met them at the airport and I was allowed to take Allison in my arms. Alison was such a pretty baby and people described her as "Gerber Baby." Her complexion was inherited from her mom and grandpa Rudi. There is so much similarity.

We visited them few times and they came once to Rio Rancho. I tried to help out with clothing for her birthdays or Christmas, which was fun for me. We know now that there will not be any siblings and she started to be very spoiled and controlled by her father. During our last visit in Pepperell we realized that there was a lack of discipline. The only thing that made us happy was that Alison is a bright girl. Being four years old, she knew the alphabet and could spell her name. The parents were reading a lot to her and getting her acquainted with all kinds of animals.

Unfortunately, we were very disappointed about the neglected house. Things were started, but not finished. After four years in the house, only windows were exchanged and both bathrooms remodeled. The kitchen cabinets were installed, but not finished, floor tile halfway laid but still partially loose. Things were dumped in corners and around the rooms.

We are afraid that this house will end up same way as Tom's parents' home. The small house was filled with collectables, items from Tom's and Mike's childhood, and even the baby clothes. Barbara, Tom's mom, cannot part from those items. I would like to describe her as a hoarder. The garage cannot be opened or closed; it is filled up to the rim.

Even though Tom's dad is in construction, repairs to his own house are hardly done. The stairway railing was ripped out of the wall at the time of the rehearsal dinner, more than four years ago, and was not fixed until now. This was confirmed by Danielle when I asked her about it.

Bill and Barbara are nice people, but common sense is missing. As I was told, everybody is afraid to say something to

Barbara. As short a person as she is, she seems to have the say-so in the household.

Chapter 30
Friends for Life

The word "friend" is for me something special and I try to differentiate between friend and acquaintance. "My friend," we often hear. I am trying to learn how close and good these friends are. For me, the term friend means loyalty towards each other in good and bad times. A personal relationship is a friendship which is considered to be closer than association. It is based on honesty, trust, and a desire for that which is best for each other.

In my life I experienced good and bad friendships. I have school friends, I have business friends, but most important, I feel blessed to have "real good" friends who I can count on one hand. Even though they were spread throughout the world, I felt very close to them. We communicated over the phone, email or visited each other whenever possible.

The following statement I recently read puts all my feelings into words:

"Friendship is different from all other relationships. Unlike acquaintanceship, it is based on love. Unlike lovers and married couples, it is free of jealousy."

Good personal friends don't cheat on each other or take advantage or lie. Also, friends don't spy or have secrets; they worry about each other, and are always ready to help.

Friendships which I cherish go way back to my school time. One of my first school friends was Marilyn. We enrolled

Ordinary Woman

in the same class in elementary school in Wroclaw, Poland. We lived in the same apartment building. Her apartment was on the second floor, and ours was on the sixth floor. We both were good students and helped each other.

Marilyn was born in January 1941 in Russia. Her parents, Mr. & Mrs. Alterwein, were in a Russian labor camp when Mrs. Alterwein got pregnant with Marilyn. The situation was not easy and the environment, with its dirt and poor medical attention, made it worse. Following the birth, Marilyn's mother was paralyzed and weak. People thought she would not make it, but she pulled out of it. However, Marilyn's father died of typhus.

Finally, in 1948, Marilyn and her mother got out of Russia and moved to Wroclaw. Before that, Marilyn's mother met Mr. Kandeszucker. They married and had a daughter Sarah.

The relationship between Marilyn and her mother was not the most sincere. I remember that Marilyn was treated as a second-level human; she was cursed and wished to be dead. Often my grandmother took her to our home and fed her. Marilyn's mother was involved in the black market, dealing with gold and money, and was imprisoned in late 1954. At that time, Marilyn had to take over the household and watch her little sister.

There was no other way but to drop out of the last year of elementary school.

In 1955 our family received the permission to move to Germany after the war. Marilyn, with her parents and sister, as well as many other Jewish families, was forced out by the Polish government. They moved to Israel in 1956. Over there she was in a Kibbutz with other young people where she also had the chance to continue her education. Later on she met her future husband, Ben Leben, who was visiting from New York. After the wedding in 1958, Marilyn moved to the U.S. where she started a family of her own. Two boys were born: Maury and Alan, who turned out very nice. Maury graduated from college and chose dentistry, while Alan preferred to be an accountant. Marilyn's parents came to the States as well. Her mother died after years of suffering with cancer, and her stepdad died many years later. She had a very estranged relationship with her stepsister, and as I just learned, they have not seen or talked to each other for more than twelve years.

Marilyn and I visited each other whenever there was a chance, but we stayed in touch over the phone and exchanged wishes on holidays and birthdays. She cared about me, as I did for her. We shared a bond that originated from the time in Poland. We are still close today, but due to the distance and different lifestyles, the closeness has diminished. We know that we are there for each other when there is a need.

In 1974 I married Stanley Pisz, a Polish citizen, and we decided to spend our first vacation in Acapulco, Mexico. We stayed in the Hyatt Regency hotel.

There we met a nice couple, Bert and Beatrice Stillman, and got acquainted. From the beginning I felt very close to them, and, as I can say today, I knew that they would be my friends. Even after my divorce from Stanley and remarriage to Rudi, nothing changed in our relationship. We are as close as we can be. When I asked Beatrice for her opinion about our friendship, she sent me the following note:

My friend Irma,
It was 1976, at the Hyatt Regency hotel in Acapulco, Mexico, when providence saw fit to bless me with the gift of Irma Bothmer in my life.
It was "click" at first meeting at poolside. We played word games (I won a bottle of tequila complete with worm), we went parasailing, and enjoyed many happy, happy hours. Along with our husbands, we toured the local markets for gold jewelry and souvenirs. We savored the flavor of Mexico at local restaurants.

Ordinary Woman

Our friendship has endured over 31 years, (and still counting..). We have shared love, compassion and momentous occasions in each of our lives.

Through all of life's challenges, like cream, Irma has risen to the top! As a caring friend, as an academic and as a courageous woman, she has, and always will, endear herself to all who have the good fortune to know her.

Irma is my sister, my confidant, my very dear, dear friend. Love, Beatrice

We saw each other many times. Rudi and I were invited to Beatrice's grandson's Bar Mitzvah, which took place in the Jewish Temple in Baltimore in 2007. In 2008 we got invited to participate at the Bar Mitzvah celebration for her granddaughter Rachael in Baltimore as well. Unfortunately, we were not able to attend this celebration in October 2008.

Beatrice never missed to drop a note and call when she had no word from me.

She always was concerned about my health or the stressful job in which I was involved.

Cute little notes were in the mail to cheer me up. I also worried when her husband was either sick or lost a job. At that time, I purchased a ticket and visited her in Florida and we had a nice relaxing weekend together.

Another dear friend, retired lawyer and Honorable Judge in Cape Town, South Africa, Colin Prest, sent me the following lovely note:

Fifteen Years of Friendship ,

Our meeting with Irmgard and Ruediger occurred in rather unusual circumstances. Indeed, an element of chance attaché to the meeting in the sense that it might not have taken place. Had this been the outcome we would have been deprived of a long loving friendship that has been filled with blessings and pleasure, and not a few surprises.

The starting point happened in 1985 when Heike, Irmgard's niece, visited South Africa as member of a tennis team from Chicago. As a family, we offered to accommodate a member of the team. As we understood it, this was to have been a person other than Heike. At the last moment a change took place and Heike came into our home and our lives.

So much so, that the following year we visited Heike and her family in Chicago. I do believe that Irmgard and Ruediger were in Germany and we did not meet them on this occasion. But the relationship between my daughter Ann and Heike deepened to the extent that when Heike married in 1991, she invited Ann to be one of the bridesmaids. Ann accepted with pleasure and in 1991 we journeyed as a family to Chicago. It was on this occasion that we met Irmgard, and it was this occasion that a friendship was born that has lasted for more than fifteen years.

When Ann married in 1992, Irmgard and Ruediger graced us with their presence. Indeed Ruediger did us the honor of driving the bridal car at the wedding. Traveling many miles and incurring considerable expenses in order to share with us an occasion of pleasure and joy spoke of a friendship.

This was not the only occasion that many miles were traveled as an expression of the depth and worth of a meaningful friendship.

In 1992, my wife Judy and I took a trip to Germany to spend time with Irmgard and Ruediger. Rudi drove a long distance to fetch us at the Stuttgart Airport. In 1993 we traveled as family, to Leipheim in Germany to celebrate Christmas with them. On both occasions, Ruediger traveled many miles to show us the sites in Germany, which were made wonderfully interesting by the phenomenal historical knowledge and his intimate awareness of the sites and places of his native Germany. But Germany did not remain his home, as he and Irmgard relocated to the United States of America.

Nor was this the end of the friendship.

In 1998 we decided to visit Milwaukee to renew our contact, and give expression to our friendship. Irmgard and Ruediger opened their home to us, and took us too many interesting places and surroundings.

A friendship can be fickle and come to an end, especially when many miles separate the friends. This has not been the case with us. Time and distance have not been barriers. There is nothing changing in this friendship, it is a friendship which is lasting, and will not be allowed to be destroyed.

Comes a birthday, there comes a greeting. Comes Christmas, there come good wishes. Comes a special occasion, the news is shared. Real friendship is forever. It is a sharing: The good with the bad; the blessings with the hardships; the joy with the sorrows. People always come and go, but friends leave footprints in our hearts.

****

I miss Colin and his humor, which always made us laugh. Ann divorced her husband and re-married happily. She has a daughter Hannah who makes the family happy and complete. Probably we will not have a chance to see each other in person, due to the distances.

One dear person I would not like to miss and honor. His name was Josef Strasberger. Josef was born in the eastern part of Poland, which belongs today to Belarus. He was of Jewish belief, and prior to WW II, as we all know, the Jewish people in Poland had been threatened, robbed, imprisoned and finally killed. It happened also to Josef's family. The complete family was transported to a Russian labor camp, later to a concentration camp and then killed by the Ukrainians in cooperation with the Nazis.

Josef, together with another imprisoned fellow, fled and hid for weeks in the woods. They managed to dig big holes in the ground where they covered themselves with branches in order to avoid being caught by the enemy. How and when he made his way to the West, he never told me. It must have been toward the end of the war.

Survivors of the Holocaust and the Jewish community in Berlin helped him to start a new life. Together with an acquaintance, Mr. Vallerstein, he started a business. An old factory that had not destroyed was obtained. There were still workable machines which were used to process cocoa beans. He started to refurbish them for production. At this point he became active in buying cocoa beans through the stock market in Hamburg. The beans originated either from Cameroon, Nigeria, Ivory Coast (Africa) or Borneo and Java (Indonesian Islands). This why Josef established an office in Hamburg and was commuting between Berlin and Hamburg.

In October 1967, I started a job as secretary at Cocoa and Chocolate Trading Company in Hamburg and we served as agents at the stock market. Josef Strasberger was our customer. He bought cocoa beans from us. The beans were processed into cocoa powder and cocoa milk, which was sold to the manufactures of chocolate.

My supervisor knew that I spoke Polish, and therefore, introduced me to Josef. He and Mr. Vallerstein invited me for dinner and we all were speaking in Polish. We became friends, but there was always a barrier which I tried to overcome. Josef never wanted to talk about the past and the lost family. This was a touchy subject; it was also a reason why he never wanted to be involved in an intimate relationship. Everybody loved and admired his gentleness and kindness.

There was a time I got sick or had other personal problems. Josef was there and helped me in any way he could. He tried to be a fatherly friend because my family was estranged. I got flowers in order to cheer me up on different occasions.

In 1970 I accepted a job as tourist guide in Moscow and later Leningrad. As often as I could, I came to Berlin and visited him and he arranged theater tickets and introduced me also to some business friends. Dinner appointments we had in the best restaurants, either in Berlin or Hamburg. He was very modest, did not have an apartment on his own but rented a room with families because he needed to be around people. Financially, he was well situated, however, he never showed it or went overboard. He enjoyed to taking me out and made me feel comfortable and at ease.

Our friendship lasted until I was transferred by the German Office of Foreign Affairs to Chicago. From Warsaw to Berlin I could always drive on the weekends for shopping and visit Josef. But Chicago was too far away. Suddenly I realized how much I meant to him; my visits lifted him up. We used to spend holidays together and went dancing on New Year's Eves. Suddenly everything had changed for him. In one way he wanted me to go on with my life, but on the other hand he was afraid to be alone. Josef was twenty-five years my senior, and his health had to be monitored after a slight stroke. This worried me, but his family doctor, Dr. Boese, assured me that there was nothing I could do. Dr. Boese convinced him to move to Israel where his only surviving niece Hella was living. He found her through the Red Cross and Jewish Community many years after the war.

Upon arrival in Chicago in February 1974, the contact diminished. Josef wished me well when I informed him about the marriage to Stanley, but never answered my letters or wanted to talk on the phone. This chapter was closed for him. I was told that he was happy for me but also hurt at loosing a daughter. First he lost his family due to the war, and then me, as his closest friend.

Twice I visited Dr. Boese in Berlin, who died in June 2007 at the age of ninety-six. He told me that Josef finally moved to Israel where he died. I talked to his niece Hella, who lived in Haifa, Israel, in 2006. She told me that her uncle passed away in 2003. He was very sick, which nobody had known before.

He collapsed at home, was admitted to the hospital and was gone after two days.

All the good memories I keep in my heart and him in my prayers.

There are few other friends whom I met in Poland during my term at the German Embassy in Warsaw. Some of them were struggling; therefore, I supported them by mailing packages on a regular basis. In 2006, Rudi and I went to Warsaw and invited all my close friends to dinner. We celebrated my birthday, but also renewed our friendship. It was a wonderful evening that I will never forget.

Conclusion

My life experience did not end with the last chapter of the book. On the contrary, it opened doors for new experiences, advantages and goals. We all learn from the past, so did I. I am a survivor, fighter and positive thinking person. I've travelled the world, met many people and cherish friendships no matter how far away my friends are. Today's technology helps to keep in touch, whether via email, Skype or telephone.

Even as a retired person I stay busy, love to be a mentor for children at school, and help adults in learning English as second language.

I feel blessed to have a happy marriage and the ability to socialize with people around me.

My motto was and always will be: never give up.

With each step I take I continue to learn.

Irma Pallas

About Irma

As you've read, Irma Pallas has done a lot of things and had lots of good and bad times. The last two decade have been good, as Irma found love and friendship in her husband Rudi. The couple live in Rio Rancho, New Mexico. You can reach Irma at: remhtob@gmail.com

Write her a note. She'd love to hear from you.

www.ingramcontent.com/pod-product-compliance
Lightning Source LLC
Chambersburg PA
CBHW051648040426
42446CB00009B/1039